MORE SHEEP,
MORE GRASS,
MORE MONEY

PETER SCHROEDTER

Ramshead Publishing Ltd.
Moosehorn, Manitoba

I would like to thank Ted Stone for encouraging me to write, and for all his encouragement while writing this book as well as for his editorial skill in shaping it.

Thanks also to Dianne Lund for creating the cover art that says it all so well and to Julie Fast for her creative insights in the layout and design departments.

Canadian Cataloguing in Publication Data

Schroedter, Peter, 1954-
          More sheep, more grass, more money

ISBN 0-9682772-0-9

          1. Sheep. 2. Sheep ranches. I. Title.
SF375.S34 1997   636.3'13   C97-901001-2

Printed in Canada

Dedicated to
Linda, my good looking partner, my wife,
for being who she is and doing what she does

and to
my father and the other shepherds
of his generation
for all their good advice.

TABLE OF CONTENTS

GOOD GRASS + GOOD SHEEP = PROFITS

A sheep operation's survival and success depend on two components, profit and low labor management. Your sheep operation has to earn more than you spend on it, even at the low point of the price cycle. In addition, the labor required to run the sheep operation successfully has to be sustainable, even at peak labor times like lambing. Based on our experience, the only way to achieve this is to organize a grass based sheep production unit.

These very simple concepts are extremely important because if either the profit or low labor component is lacking, the operation will fail. The only question is which will run out first, money or energy? This book is about how we've been raising sheep in a grass based ranching operation without working ourselves into exhaustion.

At the P&L we've been running a commercial sheep operation for more than 20 years. We began with a 200 head, labor intensive, high production cost operation in the early 70s. Over time, our operation has evolved into a grass based, low cost, low labor management system that has survived two price crashes and at least as many scary market dips. Our agricultural background was in beef cattle and we began our sheep farming career as a diversification move to increase our farm income.

Along the way we sold the cattle herd and concentrated on the sheep enterprise because the sheep consistently outperformed the cattle in earning power. Over the years, market forces and limited labor forced us to change the way we managed the sheep. Each crisis, low markets and our growing flock called for affordable solutions. Today, with my partner working full time and my part time contribution on the ranch, we run 700 ewes and the flock is still growing. We are confident that we can manage up to 1000 ewes without too much more effort.

We consider our operation a ranch not because of its size but because of the way we run it. Our animals are expected to graze for their feed and our whole operation revolves around the grazing concept to the point where we extend our grazing well into winter and begin again as soon as the snow melts. We feed hay and grain during mid-winter, supplementing the grazing when necessary, but we keep the flock on the meadows year round.

The fundamental difference between a farmer and a rancher is a mind set. The farmer brings the feed and water to the livestock and carries the manure away. The rancher takes the livestock to the feed and water giving the flock plenty of room to spread the manure behind them as they feed. In our climate, both will have to hand feed the stock sooner or later but there is still a big difference in how they do the job. The farmer will pen the stock and feed them in a winter feed yard and lamb them in a barn some time during the winter. The rancher will feed the stock out on the meadows and lamb the flock on pasture when the grass begins to grow. The farmer wants to have complete control over the livestock. The rancher insists the livestock look after itself as much as possible, including lambing. We slowly adopted the ranching philosophy over the last 15 years improving our rural lifestyle and increasing our operation's earning power. It's also made our land more productive and given us healthier, stronger sheep.

The four cornerstones of our operation are: extended low cost grazing, affordable quality winter feed, strong healthy ewes who look after themselves and their lambs, pasture lambing and effective predator control. Once these things were well in place we began to see a dramatic difference in our operation. Our costs came way down and our labor requirement fell along with the costs.

To survive on a long term basis, we have to produce lamb that can compete economically with lamb from Australia and New Zealand. To thrive we have to produce a superior quality

MORE SHEEP, MORE GRASS, MORE MONEY

lamb at prices competitive with our competition. In North America we've always produced a better meat lamb, but we have to work much harder at controlling our costs. One of the main factors driving up our cost of production is the small flock size. To get any economies of scale a sheep operation has to have between 400 and 500 ewes. Before you can manage 400 or 500 ewes you have to have a smooth running low labor management system.

North American sheep producers have to keep in mind they are competing with sheep producers all over the world. Today's consumer expects quality at an affordable price. To stay in the game, we have to take advantage of the things that sheep do best, and there isn't a better animal for converting grass and browse into meat than a sheep. We have to adopt the affordable technologies to help the sheep do what they do best, always being careful not to let our production costs get out of hand. Our flocks have to be competitive in a world where everyone does all their shopping at the same mall.

There have been far too many wrecks in the sheep farming business. Most of the financial wrecks have been in the intensive sheep enterprises where people have operated on the principle that more lambs per ewe automatically result in more profit. Many of these sheep farmers insisted, to the point of financial demise, that if they produced enough lambs per ewe they would have to make a profit. They invested in high cost facilities and provided high cost feeds in an effort to achieve their production goals. Their operating costs went through the roof and they worked themselves almost to death only to find the market had dropped below their breakeven mark. By the time they realized what happened, they were out of business. This sad scenario has been repeated far too many times and it's given sheep a bad reputation with bankers and other agricultural bean counters. Despite the wrecks, there are many people who have always known how to make money running sheep and many others who have figured out what it takes to run a profitable sheep operation. The most successful and enduring sheep outfits are the grass based sheep enterprises. The first hurdle you have to overcome is the idea that you can't do it in your area. After that it's just a matter of adapting until you develop a grass based system that works.

At the P&L, we've proven to ourselves and the bank that raising sheep can be profitable. We've studied outfits that have survived the inevitable highs and lows of the lamb market. Once we understood what sheep do best and then allowed them to do it, things got a whole lot easier.

People who are thinking about getting into sheep production should also remember that understanding the basics of sheep farming is essential before they quit their day job. There is a lot to learn and if you've got more sheep than you can manage when you start, your first mistake will probably knock you out of the game.

There are a number of reasons our sheep operation has helped us pay the bills, instead of adding to them, for almost 20 years. The main reason is that we let the sheep do almost all of the lambing work themselves. Another reason is the sheep gather the bulk of their feed by grazing and browsing. We now have our sheep grazing well into winter and plan to extend our grazing season even further.

The only reason we can graze our sheep as extensively as we do without crippling predator losses is because we've developed affordable, effective predator control using sheep guardian dogs. These dogs protect our flock 24 hours a day, 12 months of the year, at a very low cost. Our predator losses have fallen to less than three per cent from a high of 30 per cent. Without effective predator control of some type, a sheep operation based on grazing is simply not possible in most parts of North America.

Not all sheep are suited to a grass based sheep enterprise. The sheep have to be able to thrive in the extremes of the climate. They need good wool cover over their whole body, including the top of their heads and on their legs. Their muzzles should be wide for effective grazing. They need a large rumen capacity to handle the amount of forage required to stay in shape and be productive. They must have excellent mothering instincts and survival skills.

The best place to find these sheep is in existing flocks managed for grass based production. The other way is to take your existing flock and cull the animals that don't thrive under grass based management.

We select our replacements from "low labor" ewes, ewes that know how to lamb on their own, on pasture, and then look after those lambs until weaning. They know how to graze and prefer grazing to eating hay. Sheep like this let you get on with your life instead of forcing you into the role of head wet nurse and chief bum wiper to a bunch of slobbering bottle fed lambs. The same principles work with hobby flocks because the fun soon goes out of sheep farming when you're always tied up in the sheep barn. It's even worse when the ungrateful lamb that you've been nursing along for a week decides staying alive just isn't worth the effort.

Running a profitable sheep operation calls for lots of planning based on sound information, and sound practical sheep production information is not easy to find. You can probably get the low down on backyard nuclear reactors faster than you can find grass based sheep production information. Another big problem is getting information that is useful as well as practical. Most of the sheep farming information that's easy to get at isn't worth much. A lot is shoveled out by sheep promoters who want to sell their sheep breed of the year for a quick profit. The rest is written by the people in white lab coats. They seem to lose contact with the real world too often, and some of their ideas have left more than a few sheep producers bleeding red ink all over the bank account.

Some of the best information comes from talking to successful sheep farmers. Look for sheep producers who run grass based operations, people who use rotational grazing and know about extended grazing. See if you can find someone who lambs in late spring or early summer. There are a few of them in the country and if they've been around for a dozen years or more, they know their business. Some run smaller flocks, up to 200 head. Others are on a bigger scale, running 500 or more ewes. If you've got the time and know what questions to ask, you can get some solid advice on what it takes to make sheep farming pay.

My partner and I have been getting good advice from these old sheep farmers all along. Without their help we'd have sold out in the first five years. Sheep farming isn't all that common in North America and if you can find someone who's got the experience and is willing to help, you've made a real find.

Most people get infected with the sheep buying bug just about the time sheep prices are hitting record highs. They hear about someone somewhere who is making a fortune on a few acres and a dozen sheep. They take a look at their place and figure, "I can do that. Heck I can do even better than that. I'll buy two hundred." That was my first mistake. Running a herd of commercial beef cows gave us plenty of experience taking care of stock, but the truth is I didn't know diddly about sheep. My partner knew a little more, but not enough to keep us from buying 200 old ewes at the top of the market cycle.

Lesson #1. Don't run out and buy a mess of sheep if you don't know anything about them, especially when there's a buying frenzy at every sheep sale. Sheep and lamb prices, like any other commodity, move in cycles and buying a lot of sheep at the top of the cycle isn't smart. If you can't stop yourself, buy a couple dozen and have someone tie you to a tree until the market drops. If you figure you've got to buy, buy, buy ... before all the deals are gone, you're already too late. Finding quality breeding stock isn't easy, but when prices are sky high, that's when anything with a heart beat and enough energy to walk is sold as prime breeding stock.

Because we expect a lot from our flock, we only keep ewes that meet the standard and carry their share of the production load. Over the years we've learned that no matter what kind of a bargain you wrangle when you buy your flock, you'll end up paying at least 25 per cent above the cash price. By the time the first lambing is over, you'll have lost or want to get rid of at least a quarter of the ewes you bought. We figured we would beat that problem by buying high quality stock and paying the price up front, but even that didn't work out. We still ended up having to dump close to a quarter of the ewes we bought because they just didn't measure up. Now we just add 25 per cent to whatever we're paying, and we know what the darn things will cost us.

If you're serious about getting started raising sheep, the best thing you can do is become a sheep producer groupie.

Talk to people who are doing it. Take a long hard look at the grass based operations. They are the ones that endure through good times and bad. Check out the people who are running sheep in total confinement. Compare both in terms of labor, capital investment and return. Check out what breeds they're using and ask them why.

Go to sheep sales. Talk to lamb buyers, and find out what they want in the lambs they buy. Find out what time of year the market peaks, and when it slumps. Ask them what breeds they like to buy as feeder lambs, and which they prefer to buy slaughter ready.

After you've talked to all those producers and pumped the lamb buyers for all they know, DON'T run to an auction mart and buy a bunch of ewes. Stop and take a long look at your farm, yourself and your family.

Sheep fit well into almost any type of operation but you have to use some common sense. If you're on a cheap land base with lots of room, grazing is a reasonable option. If you're in country where the price of land is to the point where the only crop that'll pay is green, leafy and illegal, don't think you'll make it pay grazing sheep. Look at a lamb feedlot instead, or try to find some place where you can graze your ewes on cheap leased land.

If you, your partner and the kids enjoy chores with animals, then a lamb feedlot operation as a grain farm sideline might be a way to go. But if nobody on the outfit likes barn chores, drop the idea. Once you've answered those questions honestly, it might be time to look for sheep.

Generally speaking, buying breeding ewes at an auction mart is like buying a car at a scrap yard. Both places collect more wrecks than bargains. It's best to stay away from the auction marts until you can sort the bargains from the wrecks. There are exceptions to every rule, and the exception to the auction mart rule comes in when you're looking at reputation sales. There are sales that have been around for years, where commercial producers put their ewe lambs, yearlings and flock dispersals on the block. If you can get to those sales, you've got a good chance of picking up some good stock in a competitive bidding arrangement.

If and when you do decide to buy, make sure your sheep pasture fence is ready and you've got enough feed and water for the stock you're planning to bring home. If you don't, you could spend a lot of time hunting for your sheep in other people's gardens. Once the fences are up, be sure you know what you're buying. Climb into the pen and take a good look at the woolly critters. Get your hands on them and see if you can feel a backbone, to find out if they're skinny or fat. Toss them on their rumps, and check out the udders to see if both spigots are in working order. Make sure each ewe has four sound feet. It's also a good time to see how old they are, so take a look at their teeth.

Run your hands over the back and sides to check for cysts, ruptures and boils. Once you've checked them all out, trot them around the pen a couple of times and listen. If you've got a bunch of coughing going on, look at another pen. Many older sheep have lung problems. At the same time watch for limping sheep, it doesn't pay to take a chance buying sheep that might have footrot.

If they pass inspection, set a top price and don't go higher. If you believe the auctioneers when they say, "Now here's a fine pen of ewes," you could be in for a surprise when you get them home. If you take the time and stick to your standards, stay sober and keep your cool, you've got half a chance of taking home some decent stock.

If you've got no livestock experience at all, one of the safest ways to start a flock is with a handful or 20 ewe lambs. Organize it so they lamb at the same time the grass begins to grow. It's the safest time to lamb because the weather isn't going to kill your lambs and your ewes will get all the feed they need from the grass growing right at their feet. And you haven't had to mortgage your future to find out what sheep are like. The downside is that you will pay more per animal. Some people will tell you that you'll have more lambing problems with ewe lambs, but I don't think that is necessarily true. Lambing problems with ewe lambs are usually the result of management decisions. In the long term, if you buy the right rams, odds are that you'll have healthier and more productive sheep.

If the thought of lambing out a flock of ewe lambs is too hard to handle, think about keeping them one year without breeding them or buying open yearlings to start your flock. Yearlings may be more expensive, but they should be well grown out. They can handle lambing stress from most rams without the problems we sometimes see in ewe lambs.

If you get the right type of sheep and combine them with lots of good grass, clean water, snug fences and the right attitude, you'll never be sorry you got into the sheep business.

Farm people do a lot of talking about sheep even if they've never owned a single lamb. Most of what they have to say is based on stories they heard from someone else who probably overheard it in a coffee shop years ago. People blame sheep for everything from creating the Sahara Desert to ruining the western cattle range. For the last 20 years they've even been blamed for the decline in sheep farms in some circles. The real blame for that one should be be put on some of the government and university ag experts that have been steering sheep producers in the wrong direction. Most of the advice they've been dishing out would have us treating our ewes like brood sows instead of grazing animals. In spite of all the bad press sheep have been getting and all the attempts to turn them into wooly pigs, sheep have always outperformed cattle when it comes to turning grass into money. For anyone who doesn't believe it, just take a look at the sheep ranches in the western US. Each and every one is a grazing operation and they've been there since before the cowboys showed up and they're still there. Grass based sheep operations all across North America survived while the high tech high cost operations started up and limped along and went bust.

The truth of the matter is, the only way to make a decent living raising sheep is by grazing them as much as possible. The problems start when you get some cowboy exercising his jawbone about how sheep ruin pasture by killing the grass or how sheep farming is great for the coyote population. Then some government sheep expert will jump in and start preaching that sheep farmers, to make a profit, have to get a 250 per cent lamb crop to market. They're both dead wrong. The cowboy's full of bull because sheep have to be starving before they

GOOD GRASS + GOOD SHEEP = PROFITS

start eating grass roots, and you can control coyotes. The government expert is just as wrong because the bank doesn't work out the profit margins based on the number of lambs that come out of a ewe. They work out the profit by subtracting your expenses from your income.

The key factor in any successful sheep operation is profit. Without profit all you've got is an expensive hobby. The one thing sheep can do very well is make a profit. The trick is learning what you have to do for the sheep so they can do what they do best, converting grass and browse into meat. That means getting back to basics.

First, to give the livestock people an idea where sheep fit into the scheme of things when it comes to feed requirements, remember one beef cow eats about as much as seven ewes. This ratio may change from breed to breed but it's a good starting point. Most ewes require about 25 pounds of grass or five pounds of good quality hay per day to maintain their condition.

Next, remember that a sheep is a ruminant, she has the same type of stomach as a cow but it is a lot smaller. This rules out eating rusty barb wire, tin cans, sticks and garbage hay. A ewe has to have good hay because she can't take on and convert large volumes of low quality feed to meet her nutritional requirements. She simply doesn't have the room in her stomach. A good understanding of nutritional requirements is a very important part of grass based sheep production. Sheep are better at grazing and eat a lot of plants cows don't. Being a better grazer means you can extend the ewe's grazing season a lot easier with sheep than cattle, if you plan your production cycle properly.

The trick is to feed all the right stuff when they need it so you'd better be ready with the right stuff when they're building a belly full of lambs and an udder of milk. The cheapest place to get the right kind of feed is on pasture so the key is pasture management and timing the lambing to take advantage of the grass growth cycle. Sheep have a five month gestation period. To time the lambing with spring grass growth, the breeding begins late December on our place.

A key point is that sheep do well on grass. They don't have to be in a labor intensive confinement operation eating high cost feeds. They do just fine rustling for themselves on pasture, provided there is lots of quality feed available. But one thing is for sure, ewes and lambs will hold their own where a cow and calf would have to pack a lunch.

The cowboys will almost always tell you that sheep will ruin pasture. Sheep don't ruin pasture any more than cows. It's the farmer who ruins the pasture. If you push sheep they'll do a better job stripping grass down to the root simply because they're better equipped. Cows have to have something to wrap their tongue around before they can graze any volume. Even when they're clipping short grass, they can't get the job done as well as sheep can. Sheep always use their teeth, and if the shepherd is trying to clean up a pasture and not watching close enough, sheep can hurt the grass. Sheep are also more adaptable when it comes to hunting up feed because they've got a bigger menu to pick from. They don't turn their nose up at browsing brush to put on a few pounds.

Another old cowboy story has it that sheep and cows can't graze on the same pasture. Nobody ever says why they can't graze together, they just say they can't. My partner and I felt reckless one morning and ran about 20 cows and calves into the sheep pasture. At first we thought there might be a riot, or at least some isolated brawling, but nothing dramatic happened. In the end we got more use out of our sheep pasture. The truth is sheep and cows do very well together. If you run them together, you'll get about 10 per cent more grazing from your pasture. Cows prefer longer grass while sheep go for the shorter stuff. The best way to get the most out of your pasture is to rotate the cows ahead of the sheep. Another system that works well is to use the sheep to clear the brush and then turn cows in when the grass comes.

A lot of people say it's impossible to keep sheep inside a fence. I have to admit hungry sheep will slip through fences like commandos on night maneuvers, but sheep aren't born that way. They train for it whenever a farmer tries to cheat them out of feed. The best way to keep stock where you want them is to make sure there's enough feed for them to eat inside the fence. Traditionally that's meant a well built woven wire fence. Today more and more sheep producers are using smooth high tensile wire electric fences, easier to build and much cheaper.

Some people say it's too expensive to run sheep because you have to keep them inside all winter. Now that doesn't make any sense at all. Just imagine a big biker in his leather jacket and a skinny little old cowboy wrapped up in his sheepskin parka. Who's warmer? The poor old cows stand there all hunched up trying to keep warm while the farmer runs the wheels off his tractor trying to find enough feed to keep them going. Sheep usually don't even know it's cold and they don't need nearly as much extra feed to keep warm. When things get tough, ewes just bed down. The worst thing you've got to worry about is digging them out of snowbanks when it's over. If you're lambing in mid-winter, it's a different story. Nobody leaves their cows outside and unattended if they're calving in minus 30 weather. The same goes for sheep, but then winter lambing just doesn't make sense anyway.

Another thing that keeps people from getting into the sheep business is the old story that you just can't find anyone to buy the lambs even if you had them. That's a lot of bull. If you have good lambs, there will always be buyers. They won't come racing out to your farm for five lambs, but I've seen buyers drive a long way to look at a hundred lambs. And on the business end of farming, sheep beat cows six ways to the bank.

In our area with its 200 day feed period one beef cow converts about three and a half tons of hay to organic fertilizer. That will feed seven ewes. The same ratio goes for pasturing. Stretching reality a bit, we'll say 25 cows will wean 25 calves at 475 pounds. This adds up to 11,875 pounds of calf. Those 25 cows translate into 175 ewes. Just for fun we'll lamb them in May and say they drop 150 per cent. That translates into 262 lambs at 85 pounds right off grass. A 150 per cent lambing rate is not at all unrealistic and neither is 85 pounds. That adds up to 22,270 pounds of lamb.

Giving the cows all the breaks and cutting the ewes back to basic production, the sheep still outproduced the cows.

So why is it that good farmers will fall all over themselves trying to get into cattle when sheep outproduce them hands down (we haven't even talked about the potential income from wool). It could be the price per pound, but I can remember when lambs were selling for more per pound than calves as many times as the other way around.

Sheep do take more management skill. It takes less start up capital to set up a sheep farm, and the turn around time is much shorter. You can also build a sheep flock faster than a cow herd, because if you look after things properly you can have a 12 month old ewe lambing.

Maybe it's the coyotes that keep people out of the sheep business. I have to admit stray dogs and coyotes can be a problem, but they're not impossible to control. In our years of raising sheep we've had a couple of bad years. In contrast, we've had lots of years where coyotes were no more than a nuisance factor. If you work at it, you can keep them under control. The key for us is livestock guarding dogs and they've solved the coyote problem. Stray dogs aren't a real problem because you can get insurance to protect yourself. Once they've done damage, you can sue the owner and shoot the dog, but don't get that mixed up. You can't take a dog to court.

When the cowboys of this world can't put sheep down any other way, someone will always say sheep stink. The little fluff balls do have their own special scent, but a quick poll of city people will tell you all farm animals, including cows, stink. This may not prove my point because most country people would say cities stink. I guess it's all in what you're familiar with. There are lots of ways to run a sheep ranch. Some stink more than others, but if you do it right and take advantage of the ewe's natural grazing strength the only thing you'll smell when you're near your flock is the scent of money.

GOOD GRASS + GOOD SHEEP = PROFITS

2

PASTURE LAMBING FOR PROFIT

For us the decision to move our lambing on to the pasture was an evolutionary process. We began, like most new producers, with mid-winter lambing. When the financial returns failed to justify the effort and expense, we moved the lambing date to early spring and finally to late spring/early summer. The further we moved our lambing into the warm weather and grass growing season, the more we began to see a positive slant in the cost/benefit ratio. Our lambing date now corresponds with the beginning of the pasture season, and our flock now lambs on pasture. Each step in this lambing system evolution was driven by financial survival forces and the desire to have a rural family lifestyle that is enjoyable as well as productive.

The decision to lamb on pasture after years of shed lambing was forced on us by our continued expansion. The flock had outgrown our lambing shed and it was time to make some decisions. We could sell off some ewes, expand the lambing shed or take a big jump into the unknown and completely change our lambing system. At the time, lamb prices were just high enough to support our family and the current operation. Expecting the ewes to carry more debt just didn't make any sense. Selling down the flock didn't make sense either, because it would reduce our income and change our lifestyle, so we decided to try lambing on pasture.

Pasture lambing is a lot more than turning ewes out to lamb. It sounds a bit disorganized, but it actually requires more planning than shed lambing in many ways.

Before you try pasture lambing you need strong, healthy, well fed ewes, plenty of good grass, lots of pasture and a good understanding of how ewes lamb under natural conditions. The trick to making pasture lambing pay off is 'timing'. You have to plan the lambing to match the grass growth in spring. That way the worst of the weather has passed, and the ewes can get all the nutrition they need to lamb and to produce milk from the pasture. In many cases, the grass will provide most of the moisture the sheep need, so watering the flock shouldn't be a problem. If water is a problem, the weather should allow for portable watering systems.

Matching the lambing to the spring grass flush means you have to know when the early grass has the most growth in your area. If you're not sure, consult the local agricultural office or grassland specialist for advice. Once you've got that worked out, you have to develop some way to control the sheep so you can move them where and when you want.

Control over the flock and the ability to deal with individual animals in a pasture setting is vital for the pasture lambing shepherd. A good dog, a proper leg hook and lots of portable electric fencing are usually all that's required to control and manage a 500 or 1,000 head flock.

The first year we did a pasture drop, we found out why stock control is so important when you're lambing on pasture. In our first try at pasture lambing, we simply turned our 600 ewes out into a 40 acre field and let them lamb. When the 40 acre field was grazed out, we moved the flock into an 80 acre field and just let the lambing continue. As the flock was dropping lambs, we'd make a pasture check at daybreak and about two hours before dark. During those checks we'd dock, castrate and ear notch any lambs that needed doing. During the middle of the lambing, when we were seeing up to 50 ewes lamb a day, we'd make a third pasture check around noon.

The first mistake we made was putting the 600 head flock on a 40 acre field. It's too small for a flock that size. We should have started on the 80 acre field and moved on to the smaller field later. Another factor to keep in mind is the need for shelter. If the weather turns nasty, the sheep like to find cover in the bush or brush. If it turns hot, they'll need the shade under the brush and trees. The best lambing pastures have a good mix of open ground and brush. Most of the pasture should be open, 75 to 80 per cent, with lots of lush grass.

I do my pasture checks from horseback, and for some reason from up there it looked like we were out of control that first year. The whole thing reminded me of running as fast as possible down a steep hill, a lot of fun until you slip. My partner was making her rounds in the pick-up, and I don't think she could see things as well from there. Until the weather changed.

One of the first things you have to accept when you move to lambing on the grass is bad weather. Having accepted that, you have to learn how to deal with it. No matter how well you plan it, sooner or later you'll hit some bad weather when the ewes are lambing. The first time we hit bad weather, I went into a panic. It started off with a cold drizzle that turned into snow which came down with serious intent an hour later. Before you could say, "Blizzard!", we were out picking up the new pairs and taking them to the old lambing shed. The storm blew itself out in 12 hours, and by noon the next day, the flock was back out in the pasture and life went back to normal. We could have avoided most of the fuss and bother if we would have lambed a bit later and kept the ewes with lambs separate from those who hadn't lambed yet. That's when I decided that if we were going to keep lambing this way, we had to have more control.

We got some information from the range lambing outfits down in Colorado and Utah. We put that advice into the pot with what people in Oregon were doing. Then we added a few ideas to make the whole thing work for us.

The ewes who haven't lambed are called the 'drop bunch'. Gently moving the drop bunch forward and leaving behind ewes with new lambs is called 'drifting'. The ewes with lambs are called pairs, and they're kept in groups of 20 or 30 pairs for a day or two to allow the ewes and lambs to bond properly. The range flock operators like to drift the drop flock forward along a creek or river for a 1/4 to 1/2 mile every 12 or 24 hours to keep the ewes with new lambs separate from those who haven't lambed. After one or two days, two groups of 20 or 30 pairs are joined. By the time the pairs are four or five days old, they run two more bunches of the same age together. This continues until all the ewes have lambed and the whole flock is reunited.

Drifting and joining up groups of pairs works out pretty well provided you've got lots of room with plenty of feed and water everywhere. But if you don't have the room, you have to make some changes.

The next year we had another late spring storm hit us. We had begun to use the drift lambing system. Our new pairs were separate from our drop band which made life a lot easier. We quickly put plastic coats on the newest lambs and gently herded them into the brush. Then we went back to the older pairs' pastures, 90 per cent of them were already tucked in under the trees and out of the wind with their lambs. All we had to do was herd the odd straggler and her lambs to cover. We never did make it to two of the older pair groups before we had to shut it down, because it was snowing and blowing so much we couldn't see anymore.

I didn't get much sleep that night. I spent most of it looking out the window watching the blizzard unloading snow and piling up drifts, wondering how many lambs would make it through alive. We had about 250 lambs on the ground, and the flock was beginning to drop 30 a night when the storm hit.

The snow and wind let up just before daybreak and I was saddled up and out at first light. By noon, the body count was in. We'd lost three older lambs in one pasture where the ewes couldn't get to cover. The flock in that field toughed it out in the lee of a small brush pile and some of the lambs just couldn't make it. One of the lambs we'd jacketed had perished, and of the ten pairs born that night, we'd lost none.

That experience taught me that if we do our job properly, we can trust the flock to look after itself. The experience proved that properly fed ewes in their prime who spend all their time on pasture, where they have to look after themselves year round, develop survival instincts more valuable than 25 lambing percentage points.

There are a number of pasture lambing systems that work quite well. One of the best known pasture lambing enthusiasts has a sheep ranch in Oregon where they've got lots of rain and plenty of grass, but they don't have the room the range operators have. In situations like that, pasture lambers have developed a system of drifting the drop bunch away from the new pairs and keeping them separated using permanent and portable electric fences.

In both the range operator and grass farmer systems, the shepherd is taking advantage of the ewe's mothering instinct which holds her to within a few yards of where she started lambing. The rule of thumb is that for every lamb a ewe has, she'll stay on her lambing bed for 12 hours if she isn't disturbed or forced to travel for feed. This is what allows the shepherd to walk quietly through the flock and drift the ewes who haven't lambed out of the area where the ewes with new lambs are mothering up. Once the drop bunch is moved out, it is important that they don't come back. That's why the range operators put so much distance between their drop bunch and the new pairs group.

A portable or permanent fence accomplished the same effect. Portable electric fences work very well for this. As the new pairs get mothered up the portable electric fences are removed and the new pairs are joined up into bigger and bigger groups. A well planned pasture or range lambing system allows the ewes to use their mothering instinct with as little interference as possible from the shepherd.

Under a shed lambing system, the shepherd is constantly interfering with the ewe's mothering instinct. First, the ewes with new lambs are taken from their lambing bed and locked up in a jug as soon as the shepherd sees there is a new pair in the making. This is done to prevent the ewe from getting confused and losing track of her lambs amongst all the other lambing ewes. It is also done to prevent lamb stealing ewes from continually kidnapping newborn lambs while the real mother is busy having a second lamb. Putting new pairs into mothering pens for 24 or 48 hours is very indispensable in a shed lambing system. The ewes are crowded too close together for them to use their maternal instincts to mother up with their lambs. In a pasture lambing situation, there is plenty of room for privacy and each ewe has plenty of time alone with her lambs before she joins the rest of the flock. This time allows her to get to know the lambs, it also gives the lambs lots of time to get to know their ewe. Left in an area without distractions, this ewe/lamb bond develops quickly into a strong survival trait. By giving the drop band plenty of room and moving every 24 hours, the new pairs have time to go through the ewe/lamb bonding process without interference.

It should also be noted that it takes time for a flock with generations of shed lambing behind it to adapt to a pasture lambing situation. Culling all ewes who do not display strong independent mothering instincts will quickly turn supervised barnyard lambers into a pasture flock in two or three years.

For the pasture lambing to work, the shepherd has to make sure everything is in place so the ewes can do their job. For the bonding to take place, the ewe has to have everything she needs for the next day or so within a few yards of where she lambed. That is why it is extremely important that there is enough feed on the ground when you're pasture lambing. The new pairs are especially sensitive to this because they will be staying in one place for a day or two. If the ewe can't find enough feed or has to go looking for water, she may leave the lamb behind or it may try to tag along. Either way, the lamb or lambs are at risk if they try to move too far too soon. Making sure there is enough feed on the ground and moving the drop bunch every 12 hours or so helps ensure there is plenty of grass left for the new pairs.

Ensuring the drop flock's field is big enough is very important. The actual size depends on the amount of grass and the number of sheep. A ewe with new lambs has to be able to take in 25 pounds of lush green grass. This will provide her with enough feed and water. If you're not sure what it takes to get 25 pounds of grass, get down on your hands and knees and see how long it takes you to pull 25 pounds of grass. If you can't do it in an hour or two, neither can your sheep. If she can't get what she needs from the grass, then you have to supplement whatever she's short. In most cases, supplementing isn't practical and it is costly. The best solution is to have the ewes lambing at a time of year when there is sure to be enough grass.

It's difficult to say how many acres you need to pasture lamb a given size flock, but getting down on your hands and knees to pull 25 pounds of grass is usually a good way to learn. The amount of room depends on two factors. My rule of thumb is that a 500 ewe drop band needs at least 40 to 50 acres of room every 24 hours. Organizing where and when to move the drop flock takes a lot of planning. The shepherd also has to work out a system to combine groups of new pairs to get them out of the way so the drop band can come through the system for another pass.

Pasture lambing takes a lot of planning, but then planning takes a lot less effort and money than buildings and hired labor.

The amount of pasture space required also depends a great deal on the amount of grass available where the ewes are lambing. I've seen it where we've run a 500 ewe drop band into a 40 acre field for 12 hours and not leave a blade of grass for the new pairs. If it's a cold, slow growing type of spring, you'll need more acres to hold the same drop bunch for 12 hours. If things get to that stage, we usually put feed out ahead of the drop flock. Spreading out hay, range cubes or grain usually does the trick. We also go back to the new pairs and quietly drop off a flake or two of square baled hay with each pair to top them off. We sometimes use corn or barley if there's lots of old grass left. If the ground is pretty well out of roughage, we put out both grain and hay and make sure there's lots of high quality hay spread out long before the ewes get into the field. Spreading hay or any other type of feed while the drop band is in the same field is akin to a capital crime. It'll stir up the ewes just when you want them to stay calm.

In our situation we sometimes get a late, cold start to spring and end up lambing before the grass really starts growing. To make sure we didn't run the ewes short of feed we had to learn how to put out hay and if necessary some grain, corn or range cubes on the ground ahead of the drop flock without upsetting every ewe on the pasture. Keeping the ewes full of feed all the time is the key. That and keeping the feed truck out of sight of the drop flock is very important. This not only keeps the ewes well fed and calm but makes them more co-operative when it comes time to drift into a new lambing field. If the flock is well fed, the drop flock usually leaves enough for the new pairs. Even without putting feed out ahead of the drop flock they quickly get into the routine and move themselves as soon as you open the gate, even if they're just moving onto fresh pasture. If you've timed the lambing properly based on the normal grass growth cycle, you shouldn't have to supplement feed at all. Most of the time when we do get a late spring, we're only out by a few days so it's no big deal because the further we get into lambing, the better things go weather and feed wise.

The most important job a shepherd does when getting the flock ready for pasture lambing is feeding. The ewes must go into the lambing season carrying a body condition score of three or better. They also have to have a complete vitamin and trace mineral package in them, not in the fridge or feed shed. They have to have all their shots and deworming done in good time and without too much stress and they have to be shorn.

Control over the flock's movements is very important. We found the control we needed by using a combination of permanent fences, portable electric fences and distance. If there is a problem ewe, we usually take her and her lambs back to the old lambing shed and deal with her there. We haul them back to the lambing shed using an old truck box and stock rack that fits on our three point hitch bale fork. Other people use a little wagon pulled behind an ATV. Both systems are really slick for moving new pairs. I prefer using the unit that sits on the bale fork because you can lower it right to the ground, put in the new lambs for bait and the ewes generally follow. All you have to do is close the gate.

Culling ewes who give us a problem lambing on pasture has reduced most of the work in this area.

Other than getting the flock in good shape and keeping it there, the shepherd's work in a pasture lambing situation is usually confined to drifting the drop flock ahead and docking, castrating, vaccinating and marking new lambs and joining up groups of older pairs.

Getting the docking and other lambing work done on pasture can be a bit of a challenge. Catching new lambs on the grass isn't a real big deal if you get them while they're still too young to run far. Trying to get your hands on a flighty ewe is a different story. That's where a reliable, well trained dog makes all the difference. In cases like that most shepherds use the lambs as bait to draw the ewes in close. The ewe is far more likely to come in if the dog sits in behind the shepherd holding the lambs. With patience the ewe inevitably comes close enough to be caught by a front leg with a leg hook. Once the ewe is caught it's a good idea to give her and the lambs a matching mark using a color code or numbers. This helps to prevent mix ups later on. Once the ewe is caught and marked, the shepherd can give her a quick inspection, checking her feet, udder and general condition to see if she needs any special attention. If she does, the smart shepherd usually pulls a length of baler twine out of his or her pocket and ties the sheep to be picked up later. The lambs will stay with their hog tied ewe, so there's no worry that they'll stray far.

After seeing our first lamb crop hitting the ground out on the grass, I knew that's the way it was meant to be. The ewes aren't all stressed out and confused, they just get down to it and lamb. After the lambs are out, they get right down to mothering up. Even the ewe lambs seem to know what's going on. We had as many as 200 ewe lambs lambing on pasture in one season without any serious problems. They are a bit skittish and it's best to use field glasses to observe them if you think something is wrong.

I'll deal with weather risks and fight the occasional coyote, but I won't put our flock back into the shed at lambing. Since we've worked the bugs out of our pasture lambing system, family life remains almost normal during lambing. In fact there are lots of evenings we go out to the lambing pasture just to sit, watch, relax and enjoy.

3

HIGH COST, LOW (NO) PROFIT, HIGH FAILURE

When all the hype and high tech bull about sheep production is stripped away you're left with one basic truth, sheep do their very best work on good pastures. Over the last 30 years, the industry has moved away from this very fundamental sheep farming concept. During that time, researchers and government sheep experts vigorously promoted an armful of new lamb production concepts. They included; total confinement rearing, accelerated lambing, out of season lambing, early weaning, semi confinement and any number of combinations. All the new sheep production systems more or less removed the sheep from their natural pasture setting into a more controlled environment.

In order to work at all, these new lamb production systems require lots of cheap high quality feed, an abundance of low cost labor, large capital investment, prolific ewes and a high priced lamb market. If any of the requirements are not met, the system begins to unravel and eventually fails. Often it's a race to see which will weaken first, the market or the shepherd. Theoretically the systems should work, but when price fluctuations in the lamb and feed markets are taken into consideration, the theory begins to show some gaping holes. Shepherds using these new systems tried to plug the holes with more prolific ewes. This increased the operation's labor requirements, production costs and, in some cases, downgraded the quality of their lambs.

Long term success in any livestock operation depends on producing a quality product with low production costs and minimal labor.

The highest single operating cost in any sheep operation is feed. The most expensive feed is the feed put up by the producer. The lower your feed costs are, the more competitive you are. Having the sheep grazing as much as possible, for as long as possible, is the cheapest way to feed sheep and produce lamb.

The most common grass based sheep operation calls for summer grazing and hay for winter feed. The ewes lamb in late spring and early summer and then raise their lambs on the grass. When the grass is gone, the lambs are weaned.

As with the intensive sheep systems, there are a number of variations for grass based lamb production. The key factors are always well managed pastures, quality hay and strong healthy sheep. These factors must be in place before there is any chance of success.

Another very important production concept that fits well into the grass based operation is keeping your flock out on pasture during the winter feeding period. Flocks wintered on pasture have far fewer health problems, and seldom need assistance at lambing. Feeding the flock in a clean environment with lots of room and bush available for shelter not only improves the flock's health status and lambing ease, it also improves the pastures. By moving the feed area to clean ground every day, the flock has access to clean snow for water and the manure is spread around on the pasture where it will do the most good without the cost of hauling it. Another advantage of wintering the flock on pasture is a cleaner more valuable wool clip. It also allows the ewes to exercise and helps them develop stronger weather and survival instincts. No matter what type of grass based sheep operation you run, keeping the flock on pasture year round is a practice that pays off in many ways.

In the most common grass based sheep systems, the lambs are born in late winter and early spring, March and April. The ewes are pulled off pasture with the first snow, wintered in feed pens and lambed in sheds. These ewes could easily be wintered on pasture and penned following the pre-lamb shearing. In well managed operations, the ewes are shorn before lambing. Each ewe and her lambs go through the mothering up pens in the barn. By the time the ewes are all finished lambing and properly mothered up, the pastures are ready for grazing. The ewes and their lambs are then turned out to pasture until weaning.

With this system, producers reduce the weather risk because their ewes and lambs are not exposed to spring storms at lambing and they can closely supervise the lambing operation. It also results in fairly high weaning weights. This system is still quite labor intensive and requires considerable investment in buildings, corrals, equipment, labor and high priced feed, at least until the flock is on pasture.

Another grass based system, not nearly as common, is the pasture lambing scenario. With this system, the ewes are bred so the lambing coincides with the beginning of pasture season. With this system, flock and pasture management are the key factors.

To be successful in a pasture lambing system, the flock has to be in top condition. There is no room in a pasture lambing flock for old ewes with misshapen udders or oversized teats. Ewes that are in poor body condition will have problems lambing and more than likely give birth to lambs too weak to get up and suckle on their own. The route to a successful pasture lambing begins a year or two before the ewes actually lamb on pasture. It begins with appropriate pasture management followed by hard flock culling and a top notch winter feeding program.

The main advantages of this system are low labor and capital requirements. This allows the producer to invest in ewes instead of extensive lambing barns and labor.

The most advanced grass based system combines pasture lambing with an extended grazing program. The flock is kept on pasture year round and expected to graze until snow or weather conditions make it impractical. When it is no longer possible to graze, the flock is fed hay and whatever supplements they need on the pasture. This type of operation requires the highest level of pasture and flock management skill and should not be attempted until that level of experience has been achieved.

HIGH COST, LOW (NO) PROFIT, HIGH FAILURE

Sheep farming is all a matter of adapting what you have to what the sheep need without spending more than they can earn. In 1990, the farm press in West Australia estimated the cost of keeping a ewe for 12 months was $(Aus)21. Considering they still have to add freight to their cost before they get their lamb over here, I figure that as long as we can keep our cost per ewe at $35 a ewe or less, we'll stay in business.

Sheep are pretty easy to look after once you figure out what they need for feed, fences and pen space. Most vets can supply you with a list of vaccines, and feed companies generally carry all the salt and mineral you'll need.

The type of facilities you need for sheep depends on what you plan to do with them. If you're planning a traditional operation based on grass and spring or early summer lambing, one of your main concerns will be fences and lots of good forage for pastures and hay. If you are on a limited land base, a rotational grazing program will get you the most grazing from the land you have. It will also help a great deal at lambing, because it allows you to keep the drop band separate from the new pairs.

For my money, running ewes and lambs on pasture in the traditional way using modern technology where it fits in is the only way to make a buck in the sheep business now or in the future. I hate work, and carrying feed to animals that can get their own isn't my idea of a good time. Sheep are perfectly equipped to find their own feed and given the opportunity, sheep can graze a lot longer than people really know.

Sheep are pretty adaptable and they've been around for a long time grazing and browsing their way through all types of land. The secret to making sheep pay, once you've got enough grazing, is keeping the coyotes under control. Some outfits wean the lambs off early and put only dry ewes on pasture to limit predator losses. That doesn't make any sense because the biggest cost per pound of gain on a lamb is feed, and there isn't any cheaper feed than grass. You can control the coyote problem and protect your lambs from predators with livestock guard dogs or donkeys.

If the high tech intensive sheep operation finds a permanent place anywhere, it will be on the small farms near large urban centers where there is a strong market demand. But even under those conditions, they will still have to compete with off shore lamb that floods the market every time the price cycle peaks.

Confinement sheep farming is a tricky business and if you don't get it right, your sheep farm will end up no more than a concentration camp for sheep. For the producer, it usually ends up being a black hole that sucks up time and money until nothing is left.

If you like to work with the cute little wool balls every day, all day long you might want to consider a lamb feedlot. It takes lots of work, plenty of know how and capital, but if you do it right the pay off is just as good as a lamb producing operation.

HIGH COST, LOW (NO) PROFIT, HIGH FAILURE

4

SHEEP BREEDS AND WHERE THEY FIT

*D*eciding what breed of sheep you should be running on your farm can get confusing. Especially when every breed promoter and government expert is telling you what breed is best. The truth is nobody knows for sure because every operation is different, and every sheep producer wants something just a little different from their sheep.

To work out the answer to the best breed question, you have to go back to basics. First, decide what type of operation you want to run. Pick a system that you know you'd like to work over the long haul. Then decide what part of the market you want to sell to. Next, establish how many sheep you want to run.

Once you've thought through all of those questions, take a look at what type of sheep there are and how they fit into your plan. When you evaluate the breed and how it will fit into your operation, stick to the breed's proven basic production strengths. Understanding what the breeds were originally bred for is very important, because that is what they are probably still doing quite well.

When you look at the common breeds in the country today, you can divide them into three groups: ewe breeds, ram (meat) breeds and prolific breeds. Generally speaking prolific breeds do not work well in a grass based situation, because their management is too labor intensive and their feed requirements are too high. But they are a ewe breed, and low percentage crossbreds may work for the more experienced grass shepherd.

The ewe breeds, excluding the highly prolific breeds, are the foundation of most large commercial flocks. Usually, what they lack in body bulk and size is generally brought into the lamb crop through a meat ram's genetic contribution. There are quite a few reasons why commercial sheep farmers use the ewe breeds as their foundation stock and bring in meat rams for sires. They are hardier, live longer and are generally better grazers. They can cope with weather extremes and perform well under a grazing system. They are also very good at lambing on their own and look after their lambs quite well in a pasture setting. The crossbred lambs that result benefit from hybrid vigor and usually wean heavier and reach market weight quicker.

Some traditional maternal breeds are also high quality wool producers. Most ewe breeds have a longer productive life than ram breeds and maternal breeds are easier to manage in situations such as herding, sorting and lambing. Most maternal breeds are as dumb and docile as sheep are supposed to be. They'll follow each other off a cliff or into a river. One person, backed up by two half decent dogs, should be able to move 500 to 1,000 ewes with lambs at foot just about anywhere. Being able to herd a flock of ewes and their lambs from pasture to pasture gets to be real important in a grass based operation.

Easy handling sheep are also important when you're trying to do things like vaccinating, drenching and sorting. Imagine having to drag 150 stubborn ewes an hour through a sorting or drenching chute.

Traditional ewe breeds easily adapt to a grazing management system because that is where they originated. Given the opportunity, many ewes quickly adapt to lambing completely unassisted and unsupervised on pasture. Provided the shepherd has kept them in good condition through breeding and gestation, the maternal breed ewes quickly adapt to looking after their own lambs under natural conditions. This allows shepherds to manage larger flocks without going broke paying the hired help. The ability to manage larger flocks also helps spread capital costs and increases returns on investment and labor.

Traditional ewe breeds are easier on fences than other breeds. But then, that might have something to do with

SHEEP BREEDS AND WHERE THEY FIT

genetic selection out here at the P&L. I have been known to make freezer meat out of fence crawling sheep.

When you start looking for ewe breeds, you can eliminate anything with a black face. A crossbred or speckled face is alright, and in many cases, preferred as a grass base ewe. If you're trying to build a low labor, grass grazing type flock, it's best to stay away from the highly prolific breeds. I have yet to see a ewe with three or four lambs at foot raise them successfully on pasture. When it's all said and done, you've got about six breeds to pick from.

On the British side, you've got the Border Leicester and the Lincoln. On the North American side, you've got Rambouillet, Columbia, Targhee, Polypay and Corriedale. You could also throw in the Delaine Merino, Debouillet and Australian Merino strains, but keep in mind that Merino strains were selected for wool production and are not well known for producing the type of lamb carcass that will make much of an impression on the lamb feeder or processor.

BORDER
LEICESTER

PHOTO: CANADIAN SHEEP BREEDERS' ASSOCIATION

If the Border Leicester is anything like other British breeds, my dog Bull and I wouldn't want to be herding them on the open range. If herding isn't something you plan to do, then don't worry about it. Border Leicesters originated in England from a cross between the Leicester and Cheviot breeds. You can find them scattered all over Canada and the US, where they do very well in high rainfall areas and lush pastures. They've got a good reputation as milk producers and are considered quite prolific lambers in the ewe breed category. They make excellent ewes in a crossbreeding program, providing good size and body length. They don't have wool on the head or legs which makes me wonder about their winter hardiness for winter grazing conditions, but they produce a heavy fleece that's popular with handspinners. Border Leicester rams weigh between 225 and 325 pounds. Ewes tip the scale anywhere between 175 and 275 pounds.

CORRIEDALE

PHOTO: CANADIAN SHEEP BREEDERS' ASSOCIATION

The Corriedale is a three-way Kiwi cross between Lincoln, Leicester and Merino. They came to the US in 1914, and do well in a farm setting on good pastures. Rams weigh between 175 and 275 pounds with the ewes running between 130 and 180 pounds. They're white faced, with wool on the head and legs. They mature early, grow excellent crossbred lambs and shear a heavy, medium-wool fleece. They're fairly easy to handle and herd. They are an ideal candidate for grass based operations were extended season grazing is planned.

LINCOLN

PHOTO: CANADIAN SHEEP BREEDERS' ASSOCIATION

The Lincoln, originating in England, is actually supposed to be listed as a dual purpose breed but I've usually seen it used as a ewe breed in commercial flocks in England. They're an old breed with large frame, and do well in wet conditions. They have strong maternal instincts and are known to wean heavy lambs in multiple birth situations. They grow long, lustrous wool that grades common in the old grading systems. Rams weigh between 250 and 350 pounds with the ewes running between 200 and 250 pounds. These are big sheep and they need plenty of feed to reach their full potential. If you've got lots of grass and can get stock that's winter hardy, they might be a good choice for a grass based operation with extended season grazing.

Rambouillet ewes are definitely a grass and winter grazing suitable sheep. They have been kicking up dust all over the Canadian and American range for over a hundred years now. They make up the breeding base for most of the range flocks

RAMBOUILLET

PHOTO: CANADIAN SHEEP BREEDERS' ASSOCIATION

in North America and have earned a reputation as one of the best breeds for grass based sheep management systems. Originally developed from the Spanish Merino in France, they were imported to the US and spread throughout the open range states and western Canada.

They are described as "large, rugged, fast growing, long-lived, gregarious and able to adapt to various climatic and forage conditions". They also cut some pretty good wool and produce a respectable market lamb that grows out well and doesn't pack on the fat as quick as some of the British breeds. The rams are big enough to make the shearers whimper, tipping the scale anywhere from 250 to over 300 pounds. The ewes weigh in between 150 and 200 pounds. They are easy herding and handling, and for my money one of the easiest breeds when it comes to fences, provided you shoot the ones that jump over top or crawl under. Rambouillet excel in cold, dry, continental climates. Our flock has wintered weather as low as minus 45°C. without ill effect. We've seen the flock graze without supplementing to the second week of December in country where our first killing frost is on September 15 and the snow sets in for keeps before Halloween. They can paw through six inches of snow and know how to look after themselves when the storms blow. All they need is plenty of feed and bush for shelter.

I might be a bit biased toward this breed, maybe, because they've worked hard for us and demanded very little in return. The only place I wouldn't run a Rambouillet flock is in a coastal climate. They don't do all that well in high rainfall areas.

COLUMBIA

PHOTO: CANADIAN SHEEP BREEDERS' ASSOCIATION

The Columbia is another strong candidate for a grass based sheep enterprise. They are a pretty close cousin to the Rambouillet, and according to the experts should really be listed under "dual purpose breeds" but most people use them as a ewe breed. They were built in the US back in 1912 by crossing the Lincoln and Rambouillet. The books say they're "prolific, hardy, gregarious and good mothers with good milking ability". And most people will agree that they turn out a nice crossbred lamb. When it comes to handling and herding, they're pretty much the same as the Rambouillet except they can jump higher fences if they want to. The best thing to do with the high flyers in the flock is turn them into freezer meat.

They are not small sheep, with rams weighing 250 to over 300 pounds, the ewes weigh somewhere between 125 and 175 pounds. From what I've seen, these book weights might be a bit light for Columbias. They seem to grow a lot bigger out on the farm. I've seen rams go well over 300 pounds and ewes seem to average in the 160 to 200 pound range.

The Targhee is another American built breed that's well suited to grazing. They spliced this breed together at the US Sheep Experiment Station in Dubois, Idaho in 1926. They used genes from Rambouillet/Lincoln crosses on Rambouillet/Corriedale/Columbia crosses. The end result is a bit smaller than the Rambouillet and a lot smaller than a Columbia with a lot of the same production characteristics. The books say the breed herds well and produces lots of twins which turn into quality market lambs. The Targhee cut a heavy medium fleece. Rams range from 200 to 300 pounds with the ewes weighing between 125 and 200 pounds.

The latest breed developed at the US Sheep Experiment Station in Dubois is the Polypay. Because of its higher than average lamb production potential, this breed has to have top notch grazing to reach its full potential. The Polypay was cobbled together in 1969. The breed is actually the result of a joint effort between the Dubois station and a California breeder named George Nicholase. The Polypay breed is basically one quarter Dorset, one quarter Targhee, one quarter Rambouillet and one quarter Finnsheep. The final cross was made between a Finn/Rambouillet and Dorset/Targhee.

In its rather short history the breed has made quite an impression, earning a reputation for high fertility with commercial flocks getting close to a 200 per cent lamb crop on a once a year lambing schedule. They have a long breeding period and reach sexual maturity early, between seven and eight months. They are good mothers, with a good disposition for herding and handling. They cut a fairly good quality fleece with weights around the eight pound mark. When it comes to size, the breed is a bit smaller than some of the older ewe breeds. Polypay yearling rams average close to 150 pounds with yearling ewes averaging just over 100 pounds. Adult Polypays are comparable to the Targhee.

The meat breeds are also sometimes referred to as the "sire breeds", so don't get confused when you're reading the sheep production manuals. The most common names in the meat breeds include; Suffolk, Hampshire, Dorset and Cheviot. The Texels are also a meat breed, but there aren't all that many around yet so I won't talk too much about them other than to say they've got a reputation in Europe for being one of the top carcass producing breeds. I know I've left out a bunch of other meat breeds and I didn't do it to offend anyone, it's just that I want to deal with the breeds most people will get to see and think about.

It seems everybody in farming knows that if you want to go into the dairy business you buy milk cows, Holstein or some such breed. If you're going into the beef business, you get yourself a Hereford or Angus or something in that line. It's the same with sheep, you've got to buy the breed that will do the job at hand under the prevailing conditions.

That being said, let's take a good hard look at the Suffolks first, because they are the most popular breed in Canada and the US.

SUFFOLK

PHOTO: CANADIAN SHEEP BREEDERS' ASSOCIATION

The shepherds that put the Suffolk breed together were looking for ewes that would produce meat lambs with a good fat cover. Way back then, fat was still a good thing and so was wool. In the last 20 years, wool has dropped off the scale as far as most Suffolk breeders are concerned; they've turned the critter into a meat machine..... well most of them have. Some have just made them tall, and these guys still haven't figured out that the air between the belly and the ground doesn't add an ounce to the market weight. Beware of the Suffolk that looks like a black faced wiener dog on stilts.

Generally, Suffolk sheep are the preferred farm sheep in North America because they are fast growing, large framed, meaty animals. A mature ram can weigh between 250 and 300 pounds, the ewe averages between 150 and 200 pounds. They have a deep, thick body with lots of meat in the hindquarters. The head and legs are covered with short black hair. Suffolks, depending on individual genetic lines, can put out a lamb crop anywhere from 100 to almost 200 per cent. What they do better than most breeds is grow fast. Suffolk lambs have some of the best daily gains of any breed. It's not uncommon to see them hitting the hundred pound mark in under 90 days, if they get the right kind of feed and management.

Sounds like they'd be the ideal sheep in a country that pays top dollar for lamb, but they've got their weak points, too.

The ewes are hard to handle and tougher on fences than some other breeds. They don't flock very well, but that isn't important unless you have your sheep out on grazing projects with a shepherd.

There are other problems the breed has developed over the last 10 years or so. Different breeders have bred for bigger, longer and taller animals and in doing that, they've lost some of the breed's meat producing ability. Another big factor, if you're going to be using Suffolk rams on Suffolk ewes, is the "Spider Lamb Syndrome". It's a recessive genetic defect that produces deformed and crippled lambs. Spider Lambs show up when you mate a carrier ewe with a carrier ram. You won't see Spider Lambs if you use the Suffolk in a crossbreeding program, but your ewe lambs may be carrying a recessive Spider Lamb gene.

The other disadvantage Suffolks have as a ewe breed is that they're not as prolific as some other breeds. Most Suffolk flocks average between 130 and 150 per cent lamb drop. Suffolks will work well in a grazing operation as long as you're not expecting them to graze too long into winter. But for my money, they work best as terminal sires over maternal breeds.

HAMPSHIRE

PHOTO: CANADIAN SHEEP BREEDERS' ASSOCIATION

The Hampshires, or Hamps, are another of the big meat breeds. At one time they were considered bigger than the Suffolks, but today it's hard to make that call. The rams can weigh up to 325 pounds and the ewes weigh in between 175 and 225 pounds. Their lambing percentages are similar to the Suffolks' but I think you'd find them carrying a bit more meat than a lot of the more modern Suffolks.

Hamps are big framed, meaty sheep. They've got a black face and wool cover on the top of their head and down the legs. They are a good farm sheep, but hard to handle. You need good fences and corrals to hold them. The biggest problem with the Hamps is their big frame. It's not a problem if you're breeding a big Hamp ram to a big Hamp ewe, but it can get to the point where the only one making money on your sheep is the vet. Especially if you try to cross one of the big boys to some of the smaller types of ewes. They also have been known to carry the Spider Lamb Syndrome gene, and like the Suffolk, their lambs tend to put on fat a little too easy if you're not watching the feed ration. Hamps can fit into a grazing situation, but like the Suffolks, their best place is a terminal sire across any good ewe breed.

DORSET

PHOTO: CANADIAN SHEEP BREEDERS' ASSOCIATION

Some people class the Dorset (horned and polled) as a dual purpose breed, but that's kind of misleading. They are a good sized breed but not as big as the Hamps and Suffolks. Their lambing percentage is around the 130 to 150 pound average range, with some flocks that do better. They're known for their heavy milking ability, as well as out of season breeding. If the Suffolks and Hamps are the Herefords of the sheep business, then the Dorset is the traditional Angus.

Dorsets are a little shorter on the legs and thicker in the frame than the average black face. They're white faced and have wool cover on the poll. They should have small ears and a short neck. If they've got a lot of leg, a long neck and big ears, you can almost bet the farm that somewhere, somehow a

Columbia or Rambouillet ram has been jumping into the Dorset ewe pen. Dorsets are known as a "long-lived" breed and the age factor is important when you start looking at replacement costs. The Dorsets also fit well into grass based situations.

Dorset rams weigh from 210 to 250 pounds, and the ewes run between 140 and 180 pounds. Dorset lambs grow fast, but tend to put on fat instead of meat before they hit top market weight. If you cross the Dorset with a ewe breed or even a highly prolific breed that has problems getting a proper fat cover to finish, you could have a winning combination.

Generally speaking, Dorsets are a pretty solid breed except for the fat factor. They handle about the same as the black face breeds, so you'll need to have your pens and pastures done up properly.

NORTH COUNTRY CHEVIOT

PHOTO: CANADIAN SHEEP BREEDERS' ASSOCIATION

Cheviots are often overlooked as a meat breed, but they've got some good things going for them if you're selling your lambs before they hit the 100 pound mark. They're about as tough as sheep ever get when it comes to taking bad weather, hard country and poor feed. A Cheviot lamb is just about the toughest critter on the farm and harder to kill than a stray cat.

Cheviots are one of the easiest lambing breeds going and the ewes really do take care of their lambs. Their lambing percentage is nothing special, running up to 150 per cent. Cheviots are not out of season breeders and they don't have a great lambing percentage, but if you're looking for low labor, low management sheep that do well on grass, you should be looking at Cheviots.

They're not too tough to handle and as long as there's enough feed in a fence, they'll stay in. If you run them short of feed, they'll bust out no matter what you try. They're also flighty and you'll have to build your pens a bit higher to stop them from jumping out. You might just have to go to three and a half or four feet high to keep them in corrals.

I don't have any firsthand experience with Texels, but I've heard good things about them as a meat producer when I was in England a few years ago. They originate in The Netherlands and have heavy muscling, a fast growth rate and superior carcass quality. Their carcass quality shines in the dress percentage yield with reports from Ireland showing up to 63 per cent lean in males and females compared to 59 per cent in Suffolks. On the downside, we don't know how these animals will do under Canadian climatic conditions and grass based management systems. The problem with the breed is that at this time we don't know how much of the info on them is new breed promotional hype and how much is based on farm fact.

The most common type of sheep in the country today is probably best described as a multi breed crossbred. She's usually a ewe with a mix of two, three or four breeds. Generally she's got one or two meat breeds in her as well as a prolific breed or two, and sometimes just because the ram jumped the fence, she might have a wool sire in her background. Crossbreeding is good as long as you can manage the input well enough to predict the outcome. Once you toss three or more critters into the gene pool, things get a bit muddy and it's pretty tough to tell what type of lamb the ewe will pop out if there are too many breeds in the mix. A two way or three way cross is about all you can count on. After that things get too unpredictable.

A lot of people in the sheep business have taken a serious look at "highly prolific" breeds. There are basically three highly prolific breeds available in Canada: Finnsheep, Romanov and Booroola.

When I say prolific breed, I mean these sheep can pop out litters of three and four lambs at a crack and there are stories of up to five lambs a litter. You can start a raging argument that can last for years trying to find out which of these high performance sheep are the best, so I won't even try. But there is something that has to be put right up front on this and it's not often done when the breed promoters and government experts talk about prolific breeds. The difference between prolific sheep and the traditional breeds is as big as between beef and dairy cattle. Beef cattle are a lot more rugged and can use poorer quality roughage to produce a calf. Dairy cattle need high quality feed and lots of it, as well as a high degree of management ability to produce the amount of milk needed to make a profit. Sheep producers who successfully manage highly prolific flocks treat their sheep the way dairy producers treat their cattle. They feed them well and look after them, knowing the animals have the ability to produce, provided they receive the feed and management.

I would not choose any of the highly prolific breeds for a grass based sheep operation. Their feed requirements often exceed what grazing can provide and they are not known for their winter hardiness. They also require a great deal of labor and management.

The first highly prolific breed to hit the Canadian sheep scene was the Finnish Landrace, more commonly known as the Finnsheep. You guessed it, the breed originated in Finland and is capable of producing two to four lambs per pregnancy. The ewes are smaller than the British breed ewes and much finer boned. On average in commercial flocks the ewes weigh 100 to 120 pounds. The rams can hit 200 pounds if they're well looked after and get enough feed. The ewes can get a bit heavier too, but most of the time all their energy is used up producing lambs, and feed is the critical factor. When the

Finns first hit the Canadian market, there was some buyer resistance but as producers learned how to breed and feed the Finns, Finn crossbred lambs have found their place.

Finns are generally used in a three way cross. Finn rams are put over a Dorset, or Rambouillet or Suffolk ewe. The offspring of that cross is then bred back to a meat breed for a pretty good commercial lamb.

ROMANOV

PHOTO: CANADIAN SHEEP BREEDERS' ASSOCIATION

The Romanov breed is the latest addition to the highly prolific team. They look a lot different than your typical white fluffy sheep. Romanovs are usually dark brown or black, and they're more hairy then fleecy. They come from Russia and there is a lot of debate over how the breed originated. Some say it's a cross between a short tailed Nordic breed and domestic Russian breeds. The Russians say it's a pure Russian breed. The entire breeding process started back in the early 1700s and it's still going on today.

From what we've seen in our travels, my partner and I have come to the conclusion the Romanovs are a bit bigger and with a bit more bone than the Finns. The problem with the Romanov is that their crossbred lambs are still hitting some real big discounts in the marketplace because they don't grade well on the hook. Lamb feedlot operators don't care for them either, because they take a lot of feed to hit the 100 pound mark. Being frank, I have to admit we'll never see the day where they'll be welcome at the P&L, but that's not because they don't have any value. They just wouldn't work on our outfit. That being said, I have seen a lot of hobby flocks and small farms where these high performance lamb popping ewes have been doing a great job. They work well for people who aren't afraid to feed good feed, and lots of it. They work for people who know how to raise their product, light lamb, and have found a high price niche in the market.

We've heard of Romanovs having three, four and five lambs at a time. The ewes usually weigh around 100 pounds. Romanov rams can get to a good size, 130 to 140 pounds, if they're given time to grow out before they're put to work. As a breed, they hit sexual maturity early and are known to be in production in a year or less. Their lambs are usually born black, and reputed to be tougher than a stray tomcat.

Each type, ewe breed, sire breed and the prolifics, have their own strengths and weaknesses. They need different types of management to get the best out of them, but they all have the same basic needs to keep them working hard for you and your family.

Seeing I don't know what you want your sheep to do, I'll give you an idea of what my perfect ewe breed would be like.

For starters she'd have to have a perfect 200 per cent lambing rate, no more, no less, no singles or triplets. She'd have to weigh in between 130 and 150 pounds, no more, no less. She'd have to conceive on first service and lamb on her own in the pasture then raise both lambs without bothering us. She'd have to finish her lambs to at least 110 pounds in four months on the grass. She'd have to be able to graze well into December and start again in mid-March. On top of that, she's got to lamb at least 11 times without missing a season and clip more than 11 pounds of fine bright wool with a 60 per cent or better scour yield every 12 months.

It would also be great if she could kill coyotes and help with haying and fencing, but that might be asking a little too much considering she's got two lambs on her. My partner says I'm nuts. She wants the ewes to be a bit heavier.

For our grazing operation, this would be the ideal sheep and 600 or 700 of them would be just about the right size flock to make a living.

5

OWNER ATTITUDE AND WORKLOAD

Looking after sheep isn't as complicated or work intensive as some people would have you believe. It can be, but it doesn't have to be. When comparing it to a cow-calf operation, it does take a bit more management skill. If you approach it with the right attitude and keep the basic principles in mind, raising sheep is a lot like raising cattle, and usually more profitable. If it's organized properly, one person should be able to look after 500 to 700 ewes. A little help with lambing and haying would make the whole job a breeze. Running a hobby flock should be pure pleasure, and you shouldn't have to work yourself or your family to death taking care of 50 head or 500.

The first thing to think about when you're planning your sheep operation is your family and yourself. If your plan calls for full employment for everyone, every waking hour, seven days a week, odds are you won't last more than a year or two. If you last longer, your kids and spouse will probably be leaving home as soon as they can raise the bus fare.

Most successful sheep operations begin with the right type of 'sheep owner attitude'. Next, they buy the right breed for their type of operation, making sure the ewes are young, healthy and strong. Sheep operations with ewes that lamb on their own and then look after and feed their lambs without the shepherd supervising every step of the operation are usually very successful. One person can only kick start, bottle feed and bum wipe so many lambs. If the shepherds are spending all their time working to keep lambs alive, it doesn't leave a lot of time to take care of the farm chores and family stuff.

The shepherd's job probably hasn't changed in 2,000 years and all our technology and science haven't changed the basics of shepherding. To be a successful shepherd today, you still have to provide your flock with good pasture, clean water and plenty of winter feed. You have to keep them healthy and strong. That means learning what type of feed and minerals they need and what diseases you have to protect them from. The trick today is to find the pasture and winter feed at a price that will turn a profit.

Shepherds have to know how to control their flocks. They have to know when the sheep need high quality feed and when they can get by on a maintenance ration. The shepherd's job hasn't changed; it's just a lot more complicated today.

A Biblical cynic could say, "The glittering idols of our time, Technology and Science, and their high priests, the Agricultural Experts, have led modern shepherds into a wilderness of high priced solutions in which many good shepherds have lost their way and finally perished." I'd have to agree with the Biblical cynic, because we've been plowing through a lot of high tech bull without turning up a lot of good answers.

If you're a commercial farmer or rancher, your main objective is still to live on the land and earn a good living from the land. If you can do that without killing yourself or the land, you've got an ideal situation. Sheep can help you do that better than any beef cow. The trick to successful shepherding today is to use the science, technology and ag expert advice to make your sheep operation run smoother with lower overheads. If modern methods don't do that, you're just working to make somebody else money.

When we first started farming, my partner and I used to work for the banks, equipment dealers and pharmaceutical companies. We were farming our way on to welfare, turning most of our money over to the bank and equipment dealers. Then I had the good fortune to meet an old sheep hand by the name of Clem Kimber from Tompkins, Saskatchewan. We spent some time talking about how it all got done in his day. He told me something that's helped us make it through the tough spots to pick up the fat paychecks in the good years. He was talking from a lifetime of sheep ranching experience when he said, "Keep your sheep well fed and healthy and they'll look after you. And always remember, you can't control the market, you can only control your expenses."

Sounds simple enough, but putting it into practice takes a bit of practice.

To look after your sheep so they can look after you, you have to know what they need and when they need it, because they don't always need the same thing. There are six different feed periods in the sheep production cycle: weaning, breeding flush, post breeding, maintenance, pre-lambing flush and nursing. On our place, we keep the lambs on the ewes for four months if the grazing holds out. In other types of operations, the lambs are weaned a lot sooner and put on grain rations, and the ewes are sent back out to pasture after they've dried up. For us, the longer we can keep our ewes and lambs on the grass, the lower our feed bill is going to be, because that's when they need the most feed. You can still keep the flock out grazing after weaning as long as there is some place to graze. As a matter of fact, we now graze our flock well into winter and start them off grazing again long before summer is back.

Weaning is both the end and the beginning of the flock's production cycle. The weaning begins by cutting the lambs out of the flock. Once they're separated we keep the ewes penned or they go direct to market. If the lambs go back on pasture make sure it's well away from where the ewes are being held. If they can hear each other calling, it only increases the stress level in the lambs.

The ewes are fasted for 24 hours. Then we let them water and feed some straw or wild hay for a day or two. The idea is to make sure they shut their milk production down and a short fast usually does the trick in the fall. If you're not care-ful, weaning can create a lot of mastitis problems. If the ud-ders aren't bursting with milk anymore, you can put the flock back on some poorer pasture. If the udders fill while they're still in the pen or even after they've gone back grazing, bring the ewes and the lambs in and give the lambs another chance to suck out the ewes. Then sort them off and try again. (This is where a sorting chute pays off.) We've let the lambs back at the ewes twice over a seven day period and we've pretty well eliminated spoiled udders at weaning.

Ewes that have been raising lambs all summer need good grazing to get back into shape for breeding. Once they are properly weaned, we try to run them on hayfield regrowth. Alfalfa regrowth is the best if you can control the bloat problem. Most of the time the bloat threat disappears after a killing frost. We've found Bloat Guard very effective if you use it properly. We also pasture grass hay fields and grain stubble. With late spring lambing and a September weaning, we need a lot of good grazing to get the ewes into good condition for winter and breeding. The more condition (fat) the ewes can put on during this fall and early winter grazing, the better they'll winter and the lower your feed bill will be. There's an old saying in the industry and it still applies today, "Fat sheep in the fall is as good as money in the bank." Sounds corny, but these old shepherds knew what they were talking about.

The early fall grazing is one of the times when we count on science to give us a hand. Because we are expecting the ewes and the lambs to make the best use of the remaining grazing, we give them all a treatment for internal parasites. Getting the worms under control helps the ewes put on weight quicker because they make better use of the feed they get. The lambs' feed conversion also improves if you knock the worms out of their guts. Once the lambs are weaned, dewormed and on good pasture, they put on lots of cheap weight fast.

When we run out of alfalfa pasture, we market the lambs and check the breeding flock's condition. We graze the ewes as long as they are still holding or gaining condition.

My basic rule of thumb is that a 150 pound ewe in a three body condition score needs at least five pounds of quality alfalfa/grass or grass hay per day for simple maintenance. In most cases the forage base has to be supplemented with a pound or two of grain per day when she is in the 21 day pre-breeding, 90 day post-breeding and 30 day pre-lambing phase of the production cycle. The amount of hay and grain required may increase or decrease depending on the body condition score of the ewe. A big framed, skinny ewe may need six or seven pounds or more of dairy quality hay plus a pound or two of grain to gain enough condition to breed and produce a strong healthy lamb. The key to establishing the ewe's feed requirements is knowing her body condition as well as frame size, and feeding accordingly. That combined with understanding how feed requirements change in the various phases of the production cycle will tell you if you should increase feed, maintain current feed levels or, in some very rare cases, cut back. The best way to find out what shape a ewe is in is to put your hands on her back and see how much flesh cover she has over her backbone and short ribs.

Once you've established the general condition of the flock and decided if they need to gain condition or maintain, you can adjust feed quantity and/or quality accordingly. Make your ration adjustments slowly, especially if you're bringing down the quality of feed or increasing the grain portion of the feed. If you're increasing the hay quality and quantity, you can do that with one step and not get into trouble.

If you have a portion of the flock underconditioned while the rest are fat, divide the flock into fat and skinny sheep and feed accordingly. It is also a good practice, and in most cases essential, to keep replacement ewe lambs on a higher protein ration. Older ewes, those near the end of their productive life, need more energy than ewes in their prime. Protein is the part of the feed animals use to build muscle and generate growth. Energy is fat and that's what they need to operate and keep warm. I always picture energy as the fuel that drives the ewe's engine and protein as the material that builds and repairs it. In most cases, four or five pounds of good quality alfalfa hay and a pound of barley will provide all the protein replacement ewe lambs will need, but just to be safe, you should have your feed tested. You can get all the energy you need for the older ewes from good hay and a pound or so of barley. The key is to feed according to body condition, if they're skinny and need to be fat, feed accordingly.

CAUTION NOTE: You can kill sheep with kindness especially if that kindness involves letting the ewes eat all the grain they want. Sheep can overload on grain and die. You have to start them on grain slowly, begin with half a pound per head per day and build them up by increasing a quarter pound every two or three days until they are at the target consumption rate.

On our place, we divide the flock into two groups: the main flock, about 80 per cent, and the replacements and older ewes who need extra feed to keep up and produce their last lamb crop. We usually end up wasting a bit of protein by feeding the older ewes with the replacements, but it simplifies the feeding chores.

During the summer pasture season, the typical 150 pound ewe needs about 25 pounds of lush grass per day when she's producing milk and raising lambs. If you're not sure that your pasture can supply that much grass for each ewe, get down on your hands and knees and see how long it takes you to pull 25 pounds of grass by hand. If you get tired before you collect 25 pounds of grass, odds are your ewe is not getting the feed she needs. Remember ewes prefer short grass, two to three inches long. Long mature grass, six to 12 inches tall, is not good pasture, and ewes will often lose condition and milk production on rank overgrown pastures.

Another very important aspect of sheep nutrition that is often overlooked or dismissed as a minor feed factor is water. Sheep need between two and three gallons of clean water a day. The amount of water a ewe needs changes. The amount she needs depends on what part of the production cycle she is in, the temperature and the type of feed she is on. She can get some, and in some cases, most of her water requirement from very lush grass, but as a general rule it is essential to have plenty of fresh, clean water available for pasturing ewes. In a winter grazing situation, our flock gets all its water by eating snow. The flock also gets its water from snow during the winter feed period. This is possible because we feed our hay on the same pastures where the ewes were grazing until the snow got too deep. Plenty of clean water is especially important in the month before the ewe is going to lamb and while she is producing milk.

In our pasture based operation with its early summer lambing, we have to make sure the ewes all have access to plenty of clean snow during the pre-breeding flush. In the pre-lambing phase, we count on melt water and grass to provide the water but we keep a portable water system on hand in case of a dry spring.

We've found that during the winter feeding period, the ewes are quite content to get their water from eating snow, provided there is lots of clean, fresh snow available. To test the concept, we provided the ewes with a choice of water and snow. If they had to walk any distance for the water, more than a couple of hundred yards, they were quite happy with the snow.

The replacement ewe lambs and older ewes have access to fresh warm water all winter long. Partly because we bring them into the yards daily for their grain ration, and partly because we have to keep the waterer going for the ram pen anyway. During the summer months, the flock is watered from wells or dugouts on pasture and we've found that the sheep prefer drinking from troughs even if the water is pumped from a dugout. Sheep are fussy drinkers, and you will reduce the flock's health status and its production level by forcing them to drink contaminated water from dirty dugouts.

The least understood part of sheep nutrition is the trace mineral and vitamin component. Just like the water, salt, trace minerals and vitamins are often overlooked. People put them out but don't pay too much attention to what they are putting out or how well the stuff is doing the job. Salt, trace minerals and vitamins may be a very small part of the total ration but they are as important as hay, grain, grass and water. All the feed and water in the world won't give you healthy, productive sheep if they are short of salt, selenium or vitamin E or any one of the more than a dozen or so minerals and vitamins. Sheep have to have their minerals and vitamins to properly use the feed and water you give them. They need them to stay healthy and fight infections and diseases. A shortage can cause poor feed conversions, susceptibility to diseases, low fertility and weak lambs.

When we first got into sheep, we were losing up to 25 per cent of all the lambs born in the first week after birth. The vets and sheep specialists told us it was a management problem causing pneumonia. An old sheep producer in the region suggested we increase the amount of selenium in the trace mineral mix. We took the sheep man's advice and solved our problem without changing any other part of our management system.

Back then the government experts told us we'd have to build bigger and better sheep barns if we wanted to stay in the sheep business. Today the old lambing barn is empty except at shearing time and our ewes are out grazing well into December. They begin grazing again early in the spring starting in April or whenever the snow melts down enough that the grass is starting to show.

It's amazing how much feed sheep can find under the snow if you've allowed the grass to regrow in the fall. If they're in good shape, we'll put them on five to six pounds of average quality hay. If they didn't do all that well grazing, we'll feed them all the average quality hay they can eat, eight to 10 pounds if they're allowed to waste some. Sheep don't do well on coarse, stemmy alfalfa but if that's all you've got, feed a little more and don't expect them to gnaw on the stems for their feed. If you haven't got that much hay, feed about five pounds and add a pound or so of grain every other day.

The rams usually take more pounds of hay and an extra pound of grain per day. The only time the rams get extra rations is when we get them pumped up for breeding. The rest of the time, they're on a maintenance ration.

Somewhere between two and three weeks before breeding begins, we pour the feed to the ewes to get them in the mood for breeding. This is referred to as the the pre-breeding flush in the textbooks. Ewes on good feed produce more lambs so we feed the best hay, second cut alfalfa if we have it, and grain. They get all the hay they can eat plus a pound or two of barley. Anytime you feed grain you have to let the ewes get used to it by working up the intake in half pound increases over three day breaks. Increasing the quality and amount of feed before breeding does a couple of things. It bumps up the lambing percentage by 10 percentage points or better and it shortens the breeding season. It also helps to get the ewes ready for the coldest part of winter with a layer of fat under their fleece covered hides. This extra fat not only helps keep the ewe warm during winter, it also helps her stay safe in lamb by providing her with a built in energy reserve which she can dip into if you're feeding a bit short later on. We keep the breeding flush going for at least 34 days after the rams have started breeding. Then we taper off the flush to a gaining ration to ensure that the fertilized eggs attach themselves securely to the uterine wall.

Make sure to keep the feed level fairly high even after breeding activity has stopped. It takes 90 days after breeding for the egg to attach itself to the wall of the uterus and for the ewe to develop a strong placenta. Strong placental development is essential to a successful lambing. The size and strength of the placenta affect not only the vigor and strength of the lamb at birth, it also affects the ewe's mothering instinct and colostrum production. Underfeeding during the 90 day post breeding period can cost you a lot of lambs and reduce the survival of the lambs that are born.

After the 90 day post breeding feed period, we cut back on the grain by feeding less per day or going to alternate day feedings. Then we slowly change the amount and type of hay until the ewes are on a maintenance ration. Usually that comes to five pounds of lower quality hay with free choice quality straw or wild hay.

To make sure the ewes are getting what they need in terms of nutrition, test your feed and work out a ration. Get help from a nutritionist if you have to, but get it done right.

Some sheep producers who live in climates slightly milder than central Manitoba graze their flocks right through the winter. They supplement the pasture rations with grain and hay for the flush, and then let them rustle through the snow for the maintenance period. If you're in a position where that's possible, it sure cuts down on feed costs. We already truck our sheep to pastures, and maybe some day we'll truck them right out of our Manitoba winter.

A sheep's gestation is about five months long. Keeping that in mind we start the pre-lambing flush three to four weeks before the ewes are expected to begin lambing. If the ewes are in good shape, a two week flush will do. At this time, the ewes get five or six pounds each of the best feed we have. At the same time we work the ewes up to two and, depending on the flock's condition, sometimes three pounds of grain a day. This flush in feed before lambing does two things. Because 70 per cent of the fetus' development takes place in the last six weeks of gestation, the ewe needs a lot of high quality feed at that time. If she isn't getting enough feed from the farmer, she'll start to use up her fat reserves, and if the feed shortage goes on long enough, she begins to use up her own muscle for protein. Once that happens, the ewe usually gets sick and often dies if she doesn't abort her lambs.

If the ewe has used all her fat reserves to grow the lambs during gestation, she won't have a lot of body reserves left to produce quality milk the lambs are going to need after birth. If you try to cheat the ewes out of feed before lambing, they won't complain or run away from home, they'll just work you to exhaustion at lambing when you're trying to keep a crop of weak lambs alive.

Once you start the pre-lambing flush, it's also a good time to treat the ewes for worms and ticks again. While you've got them in the working chute, they should also get their shots for all the diseases they might run into through lambing and the pasture season. The type of shot depends on the diseases you're dealing with in your flock. Your vet can probably help you decide on the best product.

We shear three weeks to a month before lambing starts. Pre-lamb shearing takes most of the fuss and bother out of lambing. Once the ewes are shorn, we treat them for worms and give them their shots.

A few years ago, we moved our lambing date back into warm spring weather and moved our flock out to the pasture for lambing. We made the decision after years of shed lambing in late winter. Moving the flock to pasture for lambing lets us take advantage of the warmer weather and knocked out the cost of lambing sheds. It also got the ewes on high quality feed when they need it most. The move to pasture lambing also cut our labor costs and gave us healthier lambs.

The basis of every successful, long-running sheep operation is lots of cheap grazing, and we knew we could cut our costs by pasture lambing provided the sheep could find enough grass on pasture when they were lambing. The average size ewe needs about 25 pounds of lush grass a day. That's equal to about five pounds of hay when it's dried down to 18 per cent moisture.

To figure out how many ewes and lambs can graze on a given piece of ground, you can use the seven-to-one sheep to cow ratio. If you don't know how many cows a pasture can support, it's time to get down on your hands and knees to see if you can hand clip enough grass to make up 25 pounds of grazing in a day. We usually figure if we have a good dense stand of lush grass about two inches high, it's ideal for running ewes with lambs at foot. If you can get a handful every time you close your hand on the grass, it won't take a ewe long to collect her 25 pound ration. It's also good to know that when the ewes are chewing their way through this lush spring grass, they don't need water every day. Some ewes won't drink for days at a time if they're grazing lush grass.

Once the lambs are on the ground, the shepherd's main job is to keep lots of good grass in front of the sheep. You also have to keep the worms under control and make sure the flock has enough salt, mineral and clean water. The shepherd also has to protect the flock from predators. This is very important in most areas especially when the ewes have young lambs at foot. The solution for our coyote problem are livestock guarding dogs. These big white dogs are as important to us as the grass. Without the dogs we simply can't graze the flock and all the grass in the world won't do you any good if the coyotes eat your lamb crop.

As long as the flock has good grazing, enough salt, minerals, water and good protection, they'll work hard for you. You'll have time to put up your hay and spend time with your family. Before you know it, weaning will roll around and the whole cycle starts again.

I like weaning because it means pay day is just a few weeks away. Without a profitable paycheck, we'd lose the farm and probably end up in the city having to work a real job. A fate worse than death.

I know it sounds mushy but just looking over a lambing pasture at sunrise and seeing a ewe get her newborn lambs on their feet or watching older lambs gang up and race around just for fun is a bonus too big to fit on a paycheck. It's also an indicator that you're doing your job properly.

6

SHED LAMBING A GRAZING FLOCK

For many producers running grass based sheep operations, the only practical lambing system is shed lambing. For whatever reasons, they are locked into the late winter or early spring lambing season. In my opinion it is a poor second choice, but it can be made to work provided the labor and building space are both available at a reasonable cost. The limiting factor in these operations is usually labor followed by building space. The advantage is that late winter and early spring lambing allows you to use the grass to feed the lamb crop to slaughter weight on pasture without getting into a feedlot situation. The downside is the work, and knowing that your lambs will be heading off to market just about the same time as everyone else is selling their lambs.

If shed lambing is your only practical option, remember that it calls for a serious commitment in labor and building space. Two energetic and experienced people working full time at lambing should be able to manage 400 ewes, if they work hard and have a good system. They need to be well equipped and organized.

In an open front, loose housing situation, the minimal space for each pregnant ewe under cover is 16 square feet. I think this is a bit tight unless you're housing shorn ewes, in which case the ewes should have free and easy access to fully enclosed housing. In addition to the space allotment in the shed, each ewe should have access to 32 square feet of well drained and wind sheltered outside pen space. The more room you allow the sheep, the fewer problems you'll have with mismothering.

If the ewes are to be fed on a daily basis, they will require at least 16 inches of head space at the feed bunks. In a self-feed situation, that can be reduced to six inches provided the self-feeder always has feed accessible to the animals. The throat height, depending on the breed, will vary from 12 to 15 inches. If vertical bars are being used on a self-feeder, they should be narrower than three inches to prevent trapping ewes trying to climb into the feeder.

We have found that commercially made sheep watering bowls are too low to the ground and often act as a catch all for manure and feed. We have had much more success with cattle waterers equipped with a suitable step up so the ewes can comfortably reach the watering bowl. This prevents much of the waste feed and manure build up in the waterer. In a shed lambing situation, it is very important to inspect and clean the waterer at least once a day.

The drop area, usually an open front shed if you are lambing woolled sheep or a fully enclosed building for shorn ewes, should have room enough to allow 16 square feet per ewe. It should be well bedded with provisions on hand to eliminate wind and extremely cold temperatures. In the case of an open front shed, part of the shed should have a clear plastic front on it to cut the wind and increase the daytime temperature. Some producers cover the top two-thirds of the open front shed with clear plastic and hang tarps over the bottom third at night.

When dealing with shorn ewes in a winter lambing situation, it is very important that (a) the ewes be in excellent body condition, body condition score 3 to 3+ and (b) that they have constant and easy access to a fully enclosed building large enough to accommodate all the animals comfortably. It is also important to note that shorn ewes require a higher energy ration than woolled sheep. The advantages of lambing shorn ewes will offset the cost of extra feed and housing.

Inside the claiming barn, you should have 20 square feet per ewe plus room for alleys to feed, water and move the ewes in and out. The claiming jugs should be four feet by five feet with easy access for cleaning and feeding. In a well managed flock where up to 90 per cent of the ewes can lamb in the first cycle, 17 days, allowances have to be made to ensure that there are enough claiming pens or "jugs". Allowing up to 20 claiming pens per hundred ewes will usually do the trick.

For winter lambing, we run 100 medium size shorn ewes in 1,600 square feet of shed space. If they're not shorn, I'd cut it back to 80 or 85 head. No matter how you look at it, it's a bit tight in the beginning, but as the ewes lamb and move out, things ease up considerably. As more ewes have finished lambing, the drop area gets smaller and the mothering and hardening areas get bigger.

In this type of set-up, portable panels (homemade or bought) are very important lambing tools. A manure pack or dirt floor not only allows you to drive posts or steel bars where you need them, it also helps keep the bedding dry. I strongly believe that cement floors in lambing areas kill lambs. Unless you have a heated concrete floor, the lambs will always be on a cold, damp bed. The concrete floor also limits how you set up your jugs, and a flexible claiming jug setup is very handy when things are changing every day.

We like to have the shed well lit, and instead of an office or heated area to warm up lambs, we've got a couple of hot boxes with electric heaters. A hair dryer in a cardboard box will do the same job. The hot box beats any heat lamp set-up hands down. The very best way to deal with chilled lambs is to prevent them.

Divide your drop area into pens of 40 to 50 ewes opening into an alley leading to the 4'x5' lambing jugs. This lets you get the ewe and her new lambs into their mothering pen without having to walk through all the drop pens where you'd be stirring up the old girls who haven't lambed yet. It also makes moving ewe and lamb pairs a lot easier for everybody.

The drop area of the lambing barns must be well ventilated, draft free and dry. The ideal temperature in the drop barn is a few degrees above the freezing mark. There also have to be provisions for a heated area where the ewes and newborn lambs that need special care can be kept. The claiming part of the lambing barn also has to have access to plenty of fresh water because each ewe will need two to three gallons per day while she's in the claiming pen.

Once the ewe is mothered up with her lambs, they're moved into a hardening pen. This is where the ewe to lamb bonding that took place in the jug is put to a test. The hardening pens should have at least 20 square feet per pair and no more than five new pairs per pen to start. This can be increased as the bonding is proven, up to a maximum of 50 ewe/lamb(s) pairs to a pen.

The drop pen, where the ewes lamb, should also have room for at least 16 square feet per ewe with no more than 200 ewes per drop pen. The ideal would be 50 ewes per drop pen with a combined under cover and open area space of 50 square feet per animal.

Once the facilities are in place and up to standard, it's time to take a look at what the ewe needs to lamb in cold weather. There are a number of factors that have to be dealt with in order to have a successful cold weather lambing season even after the buildings are brought up to four star standards.

The most important is nutrition. Making sure the ewes are getting a good pre-lambing ration is essential, because if they're in poor shape or underfed prior to lambing, all the other management and work won't repair the damage done by a poor feeding program.

Make sure your lambing kit is restocked. Have a supply of plastic gloves, frozen colostrum, disinfectant and have a book on sheep obstetrics on hand, if you're just starting out.

Even if your drop area and lambing barn is big and warm enough for all the ewes who are going to lamb, you still have to be there to supervise the event and get the new pair into the claiming pen. This is where the labor aspect of winter lambing can begin to wear people down. Being there to help the ewe and making sure the lamb is dried off and getting a good suck quickly is essential during winter lambing. This makes knowing when your ewes will start lambing very important. Make sure you know when the rams went out, because you can expect your first lambs five months plus or minus ten days after the rams went out. Knowing all this will not tell you which ewe will lamb first or when she'll drop. Nobody knows exactly when, but you have to be prepared. Even if the ewe could talk she couldn't tell you the day or hour. But there are a few things that help narrow down the time.

Shearing the ewes before lambing cuts the guess work in half because you can see what's happening. If you're not set up to handle shorn ewes in the winter, consider shearing the belly and crutch. It's not as good, but it still opens things up so you can see what's going on. Pre-lamb shearing also makes it easier for the lambs to find their lunch and it keeps the whole lunch area much cleaner. Pre-lamb shearing also improves the barn temperature and reduces moisture problems in the lambing barn.

My partner is the lambing expert on our place. She uses the udder development as a guide to predict who is going to lamb and when. The udder is the long term indicator that lets you know you might have a week or two of sanity left. The udder sometimes begins to form a month prior to lambing, filling with milk up to two weeks before the ewe pops. When the teats become firm and full of milk, you should be into the final seven day countdown.

You may have noticed I'm sounding like a politician that doesn't want to be pinned down. It's not because I'm running for town dog catcher or anything, it's just because there aren't any hard and fast rules in this game. I'm only pointing out what to look for. Something else to keep in mind is that indicators vary in strength from breed to breed.

While you're checking the bags, take a look at the rest of the back end. As the ewe gets closer to lambing, the genital area begins to swell like it does on a cow. The amount of swelling varies. If it's extremely cold, there is little swelling. The warmer the weather, the more visible the swelling. The swelling and general change of the genitals reaches its maximum about a week prior to lambing.

Another sign that lets you know a ewe is getting closer is when the ewe takes a real interest in other ewes already lambing and tries to steal lambs. In most cases, this means she's less than a week away from popping her own. Usually she'll drop within a day or two. That being said, my partner likes to remind me of the time I spent two weeks watching a lamb-stealing ewe before she finally had her lambs when no one was watching. Each ewe has its own character and knowing your flock really pays off big at lambing. My partner knew the old boot had a habit of trying to steal lambs long before her time was due.

We've learned that you can't base your call on a single indicator. Look at the whole animal, its behavior and surroundings. As the time gets closer, the udder looks fuller and in the last 24 hours, it gets a stretched and shiny look. In that same time frame, look for the lambs to drop inside the ewe. Before birth, the lambs go down inside the ewe to line up with the birth canal. When this happens, the ewe looks gaunt and hollow up high while she's sagging a full gut down below.

A profitable time investment at lambing time is just to stand and watch all the ewes in the drop area, it's also a great way to do something important without working up a big sweat. By taking your time and watching the flock, you'll get to know them. Try not to get caught talking to them too often, it's not good for your reputation in town.

The next indicator for 'pop out time' is when a ewe begins acting out of character. This is where knowing your ewes really pays off. As the time gets closer, they'll go off feed and stare into space. They'll wander away from the flock, or just keep walking around when others are bedded down. I don't know why they act this way. For all I know they could be looking for a phone to order in pizza, pickles and ice cream.

Now we're down to eight hours or less. They'll be off feed and probably won't be chewing their cud.

Getting still closer, we're talking a couple hours now, they'll fuss and bother more than an interior decorator, trying to get their bedding area just right. They'll usually head for the lambing area where other ewes broke their water and lambed. When they do, they might spend a while lying down and popping right back up again, like some bright eyed four-year-old who can't go to sleep.

At about this time, check them at least every 30 minutes if it's really cold in the drop area.

You know you've got something happening when the water bag is out. Sometimes the water bag breaks and all that's left is a wet back end or dirty hocks, which means you have to look them over carefully.

Once they lie down and start straining, they make some interesting and unusual sounds so keep your ears open. You'll know they're definitely lambing when you see the feet poking out. Once that happens, don't panic and rush in like an avenging angel; give things time to happen. If she's been straining for 20 minutes and isn't making any progress, then she may need help.

Being right there on the spot to see the lambs being born is great and I've known people to stay up endless hours waiting for the event, the first hundred or so times. Then things settle down, the miracle of birth and the novelty of handling dripping wet lambs wears off. Once that happens, people get into the "I'll check them every hour or so" routine. An hour is a pretty long time for a wet newborn lamb that's just a bit on the weak side, and from time to time you might just have to become a first responder to keep the little sucker going.

A lot of people ask if there is much of a problem lambing out sheep and if the question comes from cowboy types they usually mean, "Do you get to use the equivalent calf puller on sheep or how can you get your arm into a sheep when she's having problems delivering?" First off, sheep don't have too many problems popping out lambs and if they do, a tug on the lamb's legs usually gets things straightened out. If you do have to get your hands into a ewe to get a lamb straightened out, you can. You can get right in up to your elbows and better if you have to, but it's a rare event and I avoid it whenever possible. We spend more time keeping lambs going after the ewe has delivered than we do delivering lambs.

I've got a big stack of hints from my partner on how to deal with most weak newborn lamb situations. The first hint is that most of the problems can be avoided by picking the right size ram for your ewes and then feeding your ewes properly. But if you've got problems, you still have to deal with them. Most of the stuff has to do with what you can do when you come across a steaming wet newborn lamb who forgot to get up or start breathing.

If you're a cowboy and you find a cold wet lamb on the way to check the cows, you'd probably offer it to your pup for a late night snack. If you're a hardworking sheep farmer, you'll get right to work. Check for a heartbeat. Put your index finger under the lamb's front legs. If you haven't got a heartbeat, odds are he's dead, but then you might just have cold fingers. Give him a quick rub with a handful of bedding or sacking. Concentrate on the ribcage. Sometimes this form of heart massage gets a reaction if there's a spark left in him. There are times my imagination has me believing I've actually push started a heartbeat. I know that can't be, but it makes me feel good.

If his engine is still turning over but he isn't breathing, check his mouth and nostrils. Make sure they aren't covered or full of birth fluid. If he isn't drawing air on his own yet, gently try priming his air pump. With the lamb lying on his side, push down quickly but gently and then let the ribcage spring back. Remember you're dealing with a fragile lamb, not some big bull calf that hasn't got sense enough to begin breathing. It's just a little lamb so don't get excited and break his ribs. If he still hasn't started breathing by this time and my partner has hold of him, he'd wished he had. She grabs him by both hind legs and swings him around hard enough to send him into the neighbor's section if she lets him go, but she doesn't.

The theory is that the centrifugal force will clear the little sucker's windpipe. I figure the little guys just get so scared their eyes bug out and they do the sheep's equivalent of "OOOOOOOOH MY GOD". Next thing they're breathing. The first time I saw her doing this, I figured I'd worked out why there weren't any dead lambs left in the pens after her shift. It looked like every time she came across a dead one she'd just wind up her windmill arm and send it into orbit, or the neighbor's field.

My partner likes the windmill system so much she usually skips everything except checking the nostrils. God help the lambs that are too lazy to breathe because they get one hell of a spin to help them get started.

It sounds like it would take a long time to go through all these steps but with a little practice you can swing through all of them including the highpower spin in a few seconds. If you've coaxed a little wind into the lamb and you can see his ribs begin to work, you've probably saved one more lamb. If he still hasn't started breathing after the spin, it might be worth giving the little sucker some artificial respiration. Even if you're the type who'd put their lips on a wet newborn lamb's mouth, I'd recommend you don't. I'd sooner save my lips for long slow kisses and sipping whiskey.

Instead of pinching the lamb's nose and putting a liplock on him the way they do in the Red Cross drill, close his mouth and one nostril. Then if you want to, you can cover the open nostril with your lips and ever so gently puff a tiny bit of air into his lungs. Remember, PUFF, don't blow. If you get excited and blow too hard, you'll bust their lungs and end up with a fuzzy balloon.

I simply refuse to kiss anyone's nose. That includes lambs' noses so I put my lips close and instead of just a tiny puff, I blow up their nose gently. You can still do damage if you blow too hard but the odds of hurting them are a lot smaller. I know it looks stupid laying in the lambing pens eyeball to eyeball with a stubborn lamb that you've been swinging around by the heels. But no matter what it looks like, you'll save more lambs trying than by looking at them. Besides it'll make you feel like you did your best.

Most of the time you should be able to walk out and find the lambs up and sucking. You can tell if they've had a good drink because their tummy bulges a bit. A lamb with a tummy full of milk looks a bit like a skinny cowboy with a dozen beer under his belt. They both bulge a bit. If the lambs have had a drink, we just dip or spray the navel with iodine, make sure both teats are open and leave the ewe and her lambs alone to mother up in a jug.

No matter how much time you spend in the lambing shed, you can still get chilled lambs. If they're really cold, so cold they should be dead, the best way to warm them up is in a warm bath. I don't like to use it unless I have to, because I've got a sneaky suspicion that a long warm bath also washes away the scent that lets the ewe know who is whose lamb. But if you're caught between a rock and a cold place, get them into a basin of water at about body temperature and gently massage them until you see some improvement or the heartbeat stops. If they come around, don't just lay the slopping wet lamb on the floor somewhere. Dry it off, get a warm drink of colostrum into it and take it back out to the ewe before you find yourself the proud parent of another bottle lamb. We usually dry them off with a hair dryer before we send them back out to the ewe. That way they don't get chilled as fast once they hit the cold air.

If all fails and you lose a lamb, you can still salvage some colostrum from the ewe. If you're lucky, you might even be able to get the ewe to adopt some other bummer lamb.

It's always been a bit of a mystery to me right from the first time I saw a little lamb scooting across a snow blown lambing pen, zooming in on his ewe's udder like a fuzzy guided missile. I've often wondered how something not much bigger than a tomcat could be born into our winters and live. When you compare lambs and calves pound for pound, there's nothing tougher than a lamb. Problem is that until they're dry, they can quick freeze in draft. So unless you want a stack of fuzzy popsicles, you've got to make sure the ewes are dropping in a lambing shed that gives the lambs a chance. I've seen lambing barns that could pass for sheep shearer's living quarters. Some people go the whole nine yards with electric heat, controlled humidity, heat exchanger, the works. If we'd had a house like that when I was a kid, I never would have left home. I've also seen and worked in lambing barns that serve as calving sheds later in the winter, and for my money I'd sooner have the latter. The survival rate in old style barns is higher, the risk of epidemics and disease is a lot lower and the amount of money you've got stuck into the operation is a lot less.

For a lamb to survive the first few hours after birth, they need a dry, draft-free shelter preferably just below freezing or a bit colder and a belly full of warm colostrum. Now don't get all upset if it's colder, because the little suckers can take it as long as they get a belly full of warm milk from the ewe and they've got lots of dry bedding.

We always shear our ewes before lambing. The ewes' body heat provides a nice warm and dry environment in both the drop area and in the mothering pens. If you've got five sheep they won't warm as big an area as 200, but they'll still warm some small enclosed section of a bigger area. It also makes it easier for the lambs to zero in on the lunch spouts. This makes it easier for the lambs to fill up on warm milk which keeps them from freezing.

We quit using heat lamps because no matter how much you do to make them safe, they're not. I'd sooner lose a lamb or two than kill the entire flock, trying to warm up a weak lamb with a heat lamp.

We used to do a pen walk every 30 minutes. If it's colder or there's lots lambing, we check more often. Walk slow and take a good look at every ewe. At night, make sure you've got a good flashlight as well as flood lights. Between pen walks, take care of chores, water and feed. Move ewes out of the mothering pens to the hardening pens. Keep an eye on the pairs as you run them into groups in the hardening pens. That's where you find out if the ewe and her lambs are really bonded. If they have, they'll be able to find each other in a crowd of five or 10 pairs.

Keep a close eye on new lambs. Make sure they have a tummy full of milk. You can learn what a full lamb looks like by watching them fill up on a good milking ewe. Take a good long look and feel the lamb's full tummy. That way you'll be able to learn hands-on how things are supposed to be.

There is always lots to do, my partner tells me, and she knows because if you don't distract her she can find enough work for three people. Keep records up to date, tag or wool brand lambs and, if you're a glutton for punishment, cut out a pen of 10 or 20 ewes every shift for crutching. If you're going to winter lamb, you've got to be there, no ifs, ands or buts about it. If you're not, you're going to have problems that always end up as dead lambs.

We've got a lambing kit and aside from the obstetrical gear like rubber gloves, iodine and so on, there's a bunch of stuff for new lamb survival. I've mentioned the hot box and hair dryer. There are also some old towels, a plastic drink bottle with a lamb nipple and frozen ewe colostrum.

We also keep a stack of lamb pullovers. Odds are you've never seen anything like it but they've saved more lambs for us when we winter lambed than almost anything else. They're easy to make and beat anything you can buy on the market.

To make a lamb pullover, cut the sleeves off old woolen sweaters, then cut four slits for the little fuzzball's legs. If you've got some long, tall, basketball player nephew or son, you can get two lamb sweaters per sleeve. Cut the rest of the sweater up into squares and sew them into tubes and you've got even more lamb pullovers.

When there are ewes popping lambs out all over the place and it's 40 below and holding, we like to give the newborn lambs a quick rubdown with an old towel then slip them into a comfortable woolen lamb sweater. Then we come back in 15 or 20 minutes to see if they've had a good drink and if they haven't, squeeze about six ounces into your pop bottle and give them a quick snack until they figure out how to get their own.

My partner, the cool pro, says there's a bit of judgment involved as to when to pull the sweaters on the lambs. If the ewe is hesitant about taking her lamb, wait as long as possible, try to towel the lamb dry and make sure it's had a good drink. If the ewe's taking the lamb without a problem, pull the sweater on him even if he's still wet and get on with looking after the rest.

We keep some old tarp scraps handy just in case it gets really cold and the barn doesn't have a lot of ewes in it anymore. We use them to cover individual mothering pens, but again the sweaters are better. There are commercial products on the market made of plastic and synthetic fabric, but the best is a sleeve from an old woolen sweater.

The one thing we don't have in our lamb revival kit is a brandy bottle. If a lamb is chilled and you give it a shot of brandy, rye or granny's homemade hooch, you're not doing anyone any good. All the booze does is increase the blood flow just under the skin which cools the lamb down even faster. If you really want to warm a lamb up fast, get a vet to show you how to use a stomach tube. That way you can get something warm and nourishing into it quickly. If you're going to have a bottle in the lambing barn, keep it until the lambing's done and then celebrate and have a real party.

As much as we enjoy lambing, we gave up winter lambing at the P&L a few years ago because we had more sheep than sheds. I was also getting tired of sleeping alone or spending my nights in the sheep barn.

I used to hate those cold, cold nights. Whenever my partner's lambing shift was over, she'd tiptoe into the bedroom and then instead of tapping me on the shoulder to wake me, she'd slide this life size ice sculpture of herself under the covers and jolt me out of bed. Believe me, even without trying I can think of better ways to wake up. Then as I got dressed, she'd tell me what had to be done where, and then just as I was heading for the crunchy cold, she'd giggle something about how warm it was under the covers. A half dozen lambing seasons like that will make any man look for a better way.

7

LEARNING FROM YOUR LOSSES

Moving your flock to a pasture lambing system doesn't mean you won't have any lamb losses. In fact you might just have a few more until you get rid of the ewes that don't know how to look after themselves and their lambs. The trick is to learn from every mistake.

If you make a mistake once or twice, it shows you're human. If you screw up 40 or 50 times on the same thing, you're screwing up Big Time. If you don't want to end up another used-to-be sheep farmer, it's time to take a long, hard look at what you're doing and make the necessary changes.

There are still a lot of sheep producers out there who accept a 30 per cent death rate in newborn lambs as part of the cost of operating. They take these losses, and keep on taking it on the chin without asking every four-year-old's favourite question, "WHY?". If you don't ask questions, you'll stay in the dark for a long, long time. The losses on pasture are generally caused by the same things that kill lambs in barnyard lambing operations.

Keeping track of dead lambs in a grass lambing situation is very important to prevent predator problems. Identifying which ewe is at fault is also important information. Every lamb that dies should be telling you something. Seeing dead lambs can't tell you what killed them; you'll have to look for the answers. You may not believe it but a dead lamb can teach you some important lessons if you pay attention.

The white coat clipboard brigade has been putting some numbers together concerning dead lambs. They say a third of all lambs that die before weaning usually chill out or starve to death. Most of them die in the first three weeks, and half of all the lambs that die in that time, die of hypothermia.

Their information is based primarily on a winter shed lambing scenario. You won't find as much hypothermia in a well fed grass lambing flock because the lambs don't have to fight as much cold weather. But for a winter shed lambing set up, I've got plenty of experience and reasons to believe the research is accurate. Dead lambs wouldn't worry me so much if my partner wasn't so dead set against living in a tent. If we lived in a tent, we wouldn't need to worry about why a lamb died because we wouldn't need the money. Things being the way they are, we have to take a long and very serious look at every dead lamb. We have to see where we're screwing up and correct it.

To find out why they're dying, cut them open. The vets call it a "gross postmortem", teenagers just call it gross. I think the best description is a "jackknife autopsy".

There are a couple of things to keep in mind before you become a sheep herding coroner. You have to be careful when you're handling dead lambs, especially if you're a pregnant woman. You may be dealing with an abortive agent on the lamb, or the placenta, that could affect you and your baby. It is also a good idea to get a vet to show you how to do a couple gross postmortems, just so you can see how the pros get the job done.

My partner and I have worked out a systematic way to inspect dead lambs. We've even built in a reward system. The first one to figure out why the lamb died doesn't have to bury or burn the darn thing. The loser gets those honors.

Keep a sharp knife and a pair of heavy duty rubber gloves in your lambing kit. I also like to see a small notebook with the autopsy stuff. A short written report on each autopsy helps you review the problems, and look for the causes. One year we were able to track a bunch of dead lambs back to a feeding decision I made three months earlier. Keeping simple written records of what you find can be a big help in planning next year's program.

Once you've found a lamb that isn't moving any more and looks dead, you can get started. If it isn't stiff yet, make sure the little sucker is actually dead, check for a heartbeat. If it is dead, take a long hard look at it. The navel cord will tell you how old the lamb was. If it's dry, the lamb was probably a few days old. If the cord is still soft and wet, the lamb was only an hour or two old. Look at the bottom of the lamb's hooves. Aborted lambs and lambs born dead have soft, clean soles. If the soft pads are wore off or there's manure on them, the lamb was born alive and managed to get on its feet. The more the pads are worn, the more the lamb walked before it died.

My partner usually cheats because she checks to see if they've got milk in their stomachs. She holds the dead lamb in a normal standing position and feels its stomach. If the stomach is empty, the unlucky little sucker didn't get a drink when he needed it.

We both consider the lamb's size because the smaller the lamb, the faster they chill out at birth or in damp, windy weather. For the next step, you'll definitely need your rubber gloves and that sharp knife or scalpel. Practice following a pattern for opening and inspecting the lamb. Follow it step by step every time you do a postmortem, and you won't miss a gruesome thing.

We begin by laying the lamb on its side with the feet towards you. Grab the upper front leg and put your foot on the lower front leg. Then, open the skin along the rib cage. Look at the ribs and pay attention to the color of the muscle. If the ribs are cracked or broken, you've got your first clue. Newborn lambs normally have a layer of yellow, brown or tan fat just under the skin. If it isn't there, your lamb starved and then chilled to death. Maybe it mismothered, or maybe you just weren't feeding your ewes well enough when they were building the lamb. If the feed ration during the last third of gestation isn't adequate, the ewes will give birth to weak lambs who have little, if any, energy to get going long enough to get their first suck before they chill out.

Next, we open the lamb from front to back splitting the rib cage. Spread the rib cage, open it so you can get a good look at what's inside. As you're doing all this cutting, take a good look at the muscle. Keep in mind healthy muscle looks like raw steak, pale muscle tissue is a sign that you might be dealing with a selenium/Vitamin E problem. Don't underestimate the damage a Vitamin E and selenium deficiency can do to a sheep operation. It almost put us out of sheep. There was a time when a quarter of all the lambs born on our farm died within 24 hours, simply because of a selenium problem. The 75 per cent left was nothing to brag about, either.

Once you've got the ribs open, take a look at the lungs. They should be pink with a spongy feel. They should not be discolored or covered with spots. If the lamb died without breathing, the lungs will be discolored and flat, looking something like a liver. If there are purple spots on the lung or sections of the lung are purple, you're probably looking at a lamb that died because it had pneumonia.

An expensive lesson we learned here is that pneumonia isn't the reason lambs die. Pneumonia may be the cause but it isn't the reason. Pneumonia only hits lambs when they get weak. Your job is to figure out why they're weak and fix it. If you don't figure that out, you'll never win a fight against a flood of lambs down with pneumonia.

If you find milk in the lungs, you probably put it there with a stomach tube. Get your vet to show you how to stomach tube lambs properly.

An older lamb that's been short of milk, and finally died, will also have signs of pneumonia. It will also be quite skinny, and you've probably seen it standing around hunched up shivering when the other lambs are warm and relaxed. Even on an older lamb, the lack of external or internal fat is a sign that it didn't get enough to eat and never stood a chance because it ran out of the fuel that keeps it warm. It takes some extremely hard weather to chill out a fat healthy lamb. A skinny underfed lamb can chill out on a warm sunny day.

You can do a quick check on the nutritional condition of a lamb that died a few hours after birth by looking at the kidneys. If the brown fat around the kidneys is gone, the lamb starved to death. In cold weather, this can happen in three to 12 hours. In warmer weather, it usually takes a few days before they starve to death. From what I've read and seen, the fat around the kidneys turns to a jelly and is used by the lambs and unless the little fellas get enough milk into them right

73

from the start, they use up this reserve fuel in a hurry. Once that's gone, they're finished.

The best way to prevent this is by making sure your ewes are getting a proper feed ration through the entire gestation period. The first 90 days and the last 30 to 40 days are critical. During the first 90 days, the ewe has to conceive and settle safely in lamb. This is greatly affected by the feed ration. This is also when she develops the placenta in which the lamb will develop. A poorly developed placenta results in weaker lambs. It also has a major effect on the colostrum production and hormone activity. Ewes with poor placental development produce weak colostrum and do not have the same hormone levels which trigger a strong mothering impulse.

When you open the dead lamb's stomach, you should find curds that look like cottage cheese. No cottage cheese-type curds, and you've probably got a starvation problem all over your rubber gloves. If the stomach is full of hay, oats or pellets, they still died hungry because it takes 30 to 40 days before a lamb develops a rumen to digest hard feed.

You may not figure out what's going on the first few times you open a lamb up, but after a while you'll begin to understand what's normal and what's not. Talk to your vet or sheep specialist; ask them to get you a book with some color pictures. Get them to do a lamb or two with you to get you started.

Some things you won't be able to change until you start getting your ewes ready for next year's lambing. Other things may just need small adjustments. A simple thing like checking your ewes more often during lambing can help. Giving them more room, or allowing new pairs more time to bond in smaller groups, can also help correct some mismothering problems.

When you've got lambs dying of starvation and hypothermia, or the ewes are mineral and vitamin deficient, you've got what the pros call "weak management" problems. It's hard to get strong management unless you identify the problems. One of the best places to start is by finding out what those dead lambs have to say.

The first step in loss prevention is to identify your ewes with a large wool brand number. The numbers have to be large enough and clear enough to be seen from 20 yards away. Brand the ewes beginning with number 1 and go to 100 then change colors and do it again until all the ewes are numbered and color coded. We prefer to put the numbers across the rump right after the flock is shorn. Make sure you're using wool safe paint that will last at least through the lambing season. As each ewe lambs, her offspring gets the same number in the same color. We spray paint the lambs because it's more convenient than branding irons. You should use an approved wool branding spray that comes in cans because they're a lot easier to carry.

In our system, a number on the left side means the lamb is a single. A right side number mean it's a twin. A ewe trailing a single lamb marked on the right side had better round up her other lamb quick, or she could end up getting a cull notch on her ear.

The live lambs also have a story to tell. If you know what you're looking for, they'll tell you at birth which ones will make great replacements and which ones will only bring the production level down and the workload up.

8

PICKING STRONG GRAZING REPLACEMENTS

A successful grass based sheep operation has to have easy access to a large pool of replacement ewe lambs that will perform well in a low labor extensive grazing system. The best place to find these ewe lambs is in a well culled, low labor, extensive grazing flock. Once you've got your flock into shape and have them lambing on grass, the best place to get your replacements is from your own ewes. Lambing is the best time to start selecting your flock replacement candidates, because that's when you see how well individual ewes are doing in YOUR grass based management system.

The whole replacement evaluation process begins as soon as we find a ewe with new lambs. The very first criteria is lambing ease and mothering ability. The ewe has to lamb on her own and the lambs have to get up and nurse without help. She has to keep her lambs together and look after them. Ewes who pick sheltered spots to lamb and move to protect their lambs when the shepherd arrives earn extra points for their female offspring.

If the ewe is doing her job properly, we then look at the ewe herself. We begin by assessing her contribution to the flock's overall performance and taking into consideration her body condition, udder shape, milk production potential based on udder size, lambing percentage, genetic background and age. Age is a very important factor because if the ewe has been able to keep up with the flock standard and she's already seven or eight years old, her offspring are a valuable genetic asset and should be kept in the flock.

Then we look at the ewe's conformation, size, wool cover and disposition. She also has to fit in with the rest of the flock in terms of general appearance. Uniformity is worth a lot in terms of marketing and flock management.

If she passes on all counts, we look at the lambs as possible replacement candidates. The ewe lamb or lambs have to show potential. We prefer twins with a good birth weight and lots of vigor. They have to have good conformation, lots of length and generally be a miniature mirror image of the dam. If they fit the criteria, they are then given a ewe lamb mark which means they'll be assessed again in the fall, just before the lamb crop is shipped to market.

A quick glance tells us what we need to know. Using the ear notches, we effectively take out the ewes which fall below our minimum production standards and identify those sheep which are pulling their weight. We also eliminate the weak producers' offspring from the replacement pool.

We can make these assessments on the ewes in the field at a glance because all our ewes carry all their general production information with them. We use an ear notching identification system which tells us a lot about each ewe in the flock. All our potential ewe lambs are ear notched to identify their sex at birth. The male lambs are not notched and neither are the ewe lambs which don't meet the criteria. On one ear, ewes carry their age notch. Different positions on the ear and the left or right ear signify different years in a 10 year rotation. The number of notches in the remaining ear indicate if the ewe was born a single, twin or triplet.

The ear notches also tell us how the ewe has been performing. If the ewe fails to perform up to standard at any time in her life, she is given a third mark indicating she has failed somewhere. If she fails to lamb, look after her lambs, or allows one or both lambs to starve, she's given a cull notch. If there are special circumstances beyond her control, she's given a warning mark. If she fails to meet the flock standard the following year, she's given a full cull mark. Ewes that develop problems such as mastitis, bad feet or poor milking ability during the grazing season are caught and marked as culls when they turn up. Lambs from ewes with cull marks or warning marks are not considered for replacements.

The system is cheap, practical and easy to work. It keeps track of all the information we need to know and it's right there when we need to know it. It's not meant to replace the purebred ROP system but it can do a lot of good all the same. It works by eliminating all the sheep which can't perform up to the minimum flock standard. Any ewe that falls below this standard pulls the overall production level of the whole flock down. If you keep cutting out the bottom five or ten per cent, the flock's overall production does go up.

The only animals we want to see with far more detailed production records are the rams. They contribute 50 per cent of the genetics to the lamb crop and because there are far fewer rams than ewes, it's far more practical to deal with each ram individually.

Getting back to the ewe and her newborn lambs. If the ewe and her lambs meet the standards, her ewe lamb or lambs are processed accordingly. The appropriate ear notches are made, the ewe lamb is docked and given a number matching the ewe's temporary lambing number. We also process the buck lambs at the same time, docking, castrating and numbering.

Once the ewe lambs have been notched as a replacement prospect, we don't worry about them again until fall. They run with the flock under the same conditions as the other lambs and their ewes. The summer pastures are their proving grounds. Once we run the lambs into the corrals in preparation for marketing, we cut out all the ear notched ewe lambs that have grown to a respectable size. Then we put them through the chute again and look them over for size, again taking into consideration conformation, wool type and wool cover. We cut out all the ewe lambs with obvious faults and put the rest in a pen on their own.

We leave them for an hour or two before we come back for a fresh look at the prospects. Then we weigh them and cut out any below 90 pounds. They go back into the pen and get another once over to see if we missed any problem cases we should have thrown out. We choose the larger ewe lambs because their size indicates that they were born early indicating a positive fertility factor in the dam. The size also is an indicator of the dam's milking ability and the ewe lamb's over all growth potential.

The only real drawback in using size as one of the main selection factors is in the case where a ewe lamb was born as a twin but was raised as a single. This would mean she had far more milk than the other ewe lambs being evaluated. It's a weakness but it's not important enough to trash our whole system and go to an individual ear tag identification system that would cost us $1,000 a year and wouldn't provide nearly as much "at a glance" practical and on site information. I'm not nearly as interested in finding my top performers as I am in getting rid of the flock's freeloaders.

Ideally, once we go through our selection process, we should have an elite group of replacements made up of twin ewe lambs out of low labor twin ewes who perform well in an extensive grazing and hay ration system. In most cases, we do. If we do compromise our standards, we do it for expansion reasons. This is when we include exceptional single born ewe lambs.

After all the selecting is done, only 25 to 30 per cent of the ewe lambs born meet our standard.

If you're buying ewes or ewe lambs, all you can really go on is what the seller tells you and what the animal looks like. You'll have to assess what the seller's word is worth, but a critical look at the ewes or ewe lambs will tell you if they've got grazing potential.

A grazing ewe generally looks like a grazing ewe. She's got lots of wool cover, including on her legs and head. This allows her to bed down in the snow without discomfort. Her fleece is dense, keeping it tight, and that keeps out dirt and the weather. This results in an easier keeping ewe who produces a valuable, clean, high yielding wool clip. She shouldn't have too much wool on her face. If she goes wool blind during the winter, it will reduce her feeding ability which will drop her body condition score. If she does have too much face cover, the shepherd will have to clip the wool off her face which increases the work load, something we're trying to avoid. She needs a wide muzzle and good teeth, so she can get a good mouthful of grass every time she takes a bite. She should have good feet and medium length legs. She should be small headed, smooth shouldered and fairly long in the body with lots of spread on her rib cage. She needs a big gut to take on the volume of feed she needs to operate properly without prolapsing. She should have wide hips and a tidy udder. Her tail should be long enough to cover her genitalia to protect her from the flies and to reduce prolapse potential.

Basically we're looking for a ewe that's 80 per cent guts and ribs, supported on strong legs and feet, led by a wide muzzled, small head and trailed by a set of wide hips holding up a tidy udder. Every time we find one, we get a great, easy keeping grass converter that produces quality lambs all on her own.

THE GRAZING FLOCK'S HEALTH PROGRAM

Flock health is far more than antibiotics, vaccines and treatment methods. If the shepherd is dependent entirely on these, they've already lost the battle. To win the flock health battle and run a profitable grass based sheep enterprise, you have to approach the health issue from a total flock perspective. You can't keep 500, 600, or 1,000 ewes healthy running around with a needle and a bottle of antibiotics. At that point, all you're doing is patching up problems.

A large healthy flock is a difficult goal to achieve but it can be done even if you're starting out with a flock that has problems. But the shepherd has to understand the difference between total flock health and individual sheep health. It's the sheep producer's job to keep the flock healthy. It's the vet's job to treat sick individuals and the idea is not to give the vet any business. Most of the time the old saying, "A sick sheep is a dead sheep", is still pretty close to true, but experience lets you spot the sick ones before they become obvious to the less experienced.

Every sheep operation has some type of health program. For some shepherds, it's treating individual sheep as they turn up sick. Others are focused on total flock health, using vaccination and deworming programs on a regular basis. Our operation fell into the second category until we got tired of death losses, poor lambing rates, low lamb survival and all the work that goes with sick sheep. We didn't start making headway until we began using a simultaneous three pronged approach.

First, we made sure our feeding program, including minerals, was up to speed. At the same time, we tackled the disease prevention problems with a comprehensive vaccination program, and finally, we began to cull without mercy. If you fail to carry through on any one of the three, you'll end up defeating yourself.

Today, our feed and health prevention programs are pretty solid so our culling policy is simple: take no prisoners and ship the weak. It means that we get rid of the problem cases as soon as they show themselves. To get a healthy production flock, it helps if you start with healthy sheep, but that is just about impossible. Accepting that, it's still not an impossible situation if you take an organized approach and focus on flock health instead of treating individuals.

The first thing we did was cull any obvious problem cases. Our first hard cull came right after weaning. We checked the teeth and udders on every ewe and looked them over for obvious body defects as well as caseous lymphadenitis cysts. Any ewe with problems or the suspicion of a problem in any area was culled. This weaning time inspection and cull occurs every year now.

I've worked out a fairly simple system to check health status of individuals in the flock. I begin with a two mile quick march before we begin our inspection. I know that over that distance any weak ewe will fall behind and eventually drop out of the flock. These stragglers are cut out even before we begin the hands-on part of the inspection. Then we go through the flock and check for bad bags, lumps and teeth problems. We also do a body condition score on each ewe at this time. If the ewe is well below the flock average, she'll be cut out for closer inspection. If she doesn't have a good excuse like two extra heavy weight lambs or a worm load, she'll be culled. Our theory is that if she can't keep up, she can't stay.

We still treat individual sheep when they do get sick, but once a ewe turns up sick she'd better have a very good reason or she's on the next truck heading for town.

We also keep a close eye on the flock through the winter feeding period. We mark ewes who have problems keeping in shape while the rest of the flock is holding in good shape. These sheep are also culled, or brought in for extra feed and culled after they've raised their lambs. We have considered culling all ewes once they hit a certain age, six, seven or eight years old, but decided against it because if you cull hard enough, any animal that keeps up is a valuable genetic asset to the flock.

There are some diseases, like Johne's Disease, Ovine Progressive Pneumonia or Caseous Lymphadenitis, that call for immediate action. Once spotted, the affected animal should be culled because it is the only practical way to deal with the problem. In the case of Johne's, cull immediately because these animals contaminate the feed area and infect others with this slow wasting disease. With Caseous, cull the animals as soon as they've weaned their lambs if they are displaying external lumps and cysts. With OPP, cull as soon as the affected animal is spotted. There is no practical treatment available for Johne's or OPP. You can get a vaccine to protect uninfected animals against Caseous, but it does not cure ewes already infected.

Identifying infected ewes and culling them is the only way to deal with most of these problems. The cost of treatment is high and if the affected animals are allowed to remain on the property, they will only infect others in the flock. In the long run, treating these and other weak ewes will cost you more in cash and work than they could possibly earn.

The long term benefit from extremely hard culling is that our labor requirements and vet supply costs have gone down dramatically. Our on-farm deaths are almost none and the flock is also easier to manage when it comes to planning feed rations because the feed requirements are uniform. The exception on the feed question is the replacement ewe lamb flock. They get a special ration allowing them to grow out properly.

The key to a successful culling program is to cull at the first sign of trouble. Don't wait until the ewe is down or so far gone that she's just a wool covered bone rack. When she gets to that stage, she's of no value to anyone and an embarrassment to the industry. She might even end up as the poster sheep for the animal rights terrorists. Too many shepherds are afraid to cull hard because they think they may be selling ewes that could produce another lamb or two if they baby them a bit. If she does last and lambs, odds are her lamb won't amount to much. She'll probably be a worthless wreck by the time she's raised the lamb, and the net result will be one or two scrawny lambs and a worthless cull. What those shepherds fail to see is that they could be getting lambs from healthy ewes without the extra work or feed with the added bonus of selling their culls at a reasonable price.

All the culling this side of sunrise won't help your flock if you're not feeding them properly. Nutrition is a bit like economics; it's not a science and it isn't an art. It's a bit of both. When it comes to feeding sheep you have to understand the science before you can practice the art. The science is pretty straight forward. Sheep have basic nutritional requirements that vary depending on their size, body condition, weather and phases of the production cycle. The requirements also vary between breeds to a degree. The key fact to remember when it comes to nutrition is that a ewe will only utilize the feed available to the first limiting factor. A simple example of this would be that no matter how much hay and grain you put in front of a ewe, she'll eventually die if she doesn't get water. In this case, water is the first limiting factor. Yes, water is part of a ewe's nutritional requirement and so are trace minerals and vitamins.

The amount of salt, minerals and vitamins required varies, depending what the sheep are able to get out of the water and feed. There is an ongoing debate among animal nutritionists about how much a ewe needs of any given mineral and vitamin with most using the figures put forward by the American National Research Council. The NRC recommendations are based on minimal requirements for healthy sheep. We have found that by custom blending a salt, mineral and vitamin mix for our flock with rates exceeding NRC recommendations, our flock health and production has improved. We are currently using a blend based on a formula put together by Trevor Jones from Fairview, Alberta. The mix costs more than an off the shelf salt/mineral mix but it far exceeded our expectations with results. We have noticed a shorter breeding season, fewer individuals turning up sick and a generally healthier flock.

The best way to find out what your sheep need is to check what is actually in the feed they are eating and then supplement as required. You can get some of this information by doing tests on the grass, hay, grain and water. When you're messing around with the mineral and vitamin part of the ration always, always, get professional help. And make sure you get professional help that knows about sheep. If you try this on your own, you could poison your whole flock. When you're buying off the shelf mineral, make sure you don't buy cattle mineral because the copper content is high enough to hurt sheep.

One of the best books on sheep nutrition for sheep producers in Canada is the "Nutrition Guide for B.C. Sheep Producers" written by B.D. (Steve) Mason and published by the B.C. Ministry of Agriculture and Foods.

The third part of our flock health program is prevention. A good prevention program has three key components: corrals, timing and the appropriate vaccine. The actual prevention usually comes in the form of vaccines, but it is very difficult to get the job done, and done on time, if you don't have good corrals and chutes to do the job. The type and number of vaccines your flock needs depends on the types of diseases your sheep are exposed to. You and your vet will be the best people to decide that. You will need the standard clostridial vaccines with the first shot eight weeks before lambing and the second two weeks before lambing. If you are on an ongoing clostridial vaccination program, your mature ewes need only one shot two weeks before lambing. Your replacements should be getting two shots. Many producers also vaccinate their lambs with a clostridial shot at 10 to 12 weeks of age. You may also need to give your sheep a shot for Vibrio and Enzootic abortions or footrot.

Again, timing and facilities are very important because the job has to be done and it has to be done at the right time. We found that as soon as we had a good working corral and decent automatic syringes, we were vaccinating the sheep when we were supposed to, instead of when we got around to it.

Another part of the prevention program is deworming. Ewes and lambs carrying a load of internal parasites aren't healthy or productive. Again, timing is more important than the product you choose to do the job.

One of the best books on flock health and very basic production information from the producer's viewpoint is the "Alberta Sheep Production Manual". Some of the older editions are a bit outdated but they provide producers with an excellent starting point, especially when trying to plan a health program for their flock. It is also an excellent trouble shooting and diagnosing aid for producers trying to explain problems to their vets. The book is so good that it sometimes frightens new producers right out of the business with its long list of sheep diseases and symptoms.

We found another very important and effective disease prevention practice is to make sure your sheep are not crowded. Crowding sheep into pens with massive manure packs or muddy conditions is not going to help you keep your flock healthy. In fact, it will probably double your health problems. Give your sheep lots of room on clean, well drained ground. Keep them out on the pasture year round and you'll see a dramatic difference.

We winter our 700 head flock on the pastures near our home place. During the winter feed period, we look for areas that are well sheltered from the prevailing winds but still have lots of open space. I try to select areas that will benefit from the manure and animal activity. Rocky ridges and brush covered sections turn into very productive summer pasture after sheep have wintered on them.

The sheep stay on this wintering ground for 60 or 70 days in mid-winter. For the rest of the hay feeding period, we allow them to drift where they want on the home section and take the feed to them. Whenever possible, we spread the hay on clean snow. Sometimes the snow gets 12 or 14 inches deep, but that doesn't seem to bother the ewes when it comes to feeding. They plow right in and feed, scooping up the odd mouthful of snow to get their water as they munch on the hay. I've also noticed the flock cleans up much better when the hay is spread on clean snow instead of a manure pack. The important thing is to keep the flock out of the wind while they're feeding. If you feed them in an exposed area, they rush their feeding and won't eat as much as they should, which is the same as not feeding them enough.

Since we moved to this wintering system, we've noticed a drop in disease problems that usually show up in more mature sheep. It also lets us spot weak sheep before they become a liability. Moving the winter feeding operation to the pasture eliminates our corral cleaning bill because the ewes spread the manure for us as we feed. Feeding the flock on sheltered pastures instead of the traditional winter feed pens has some very important health and management benefits. The sheep are physically much stronger, far healthier and more self reliant when they're allowed to stay in their natural setting.

10

NUTRITION THE KEY TO SHEEP RANCHING SUCCESS

The longer we run sheep, the more I see nutrition as the key element to a successful operation. Nutrition directly affects every aspect of a sheep operation. It will make or break the flock's performance. If the nutrition is weak, it increases the workload on the people the flock is supposed to support.

One of the quickest ways to go broke raising sheep is to shortchange sheep on their feed. The other fast track to ruination is to spend too much money on the feed you do give them. It's a no-win situation until you take a good hard look at the grazing option. Organizing your sheep operation around a well planned grazing system provides the flock with the highest quality feed at the lowest cost for the longest possible time. The key to getting the most out of a grazing operation is to time the peak feed demand time with the peak feed availability. The high point in feed demand is just before lambing, at lambing and when the ewe is milking. The peak of feed availability is in late spring and early summer. Lambing at this time of year also frees up capital that would otherwise be tied up in lambing sheds. This money can now be used to increase the flock, instead of standing around idle most of the year.

If you time it so your ewes are lambing when the grass really gets going, the only time the shepherd has to provide lots of high quality feed is just before lambing. With the exception of mid-winter, the ewe can get the bulk of her feed from grazing. If the grazing is properly managed and the ewes come into the winter feed period carrying lots of fat, as they should be, even the mid-winter period shouldn't be as big a nutritional demand time as lambing. The flock does need more than maintenance in the pre-breeding flush and the 90 days after the start of breeding when the newly fertilized eggs attach themselves to the uterine wall and the ewes develop their placenta.

Any nutritional stress or shortfall during this time will result in a lower lambing percentage because fewer fertilized eggs will remain attached. Poor body condition combined with continued poor nutrition during this 90-day post-breeding period will also result in poor colostrum and milk, weak lambs and a ewe with poor mothering instincts. Ewes who do not receive adequate nutrition during the 90-day post-breeding period do not develop a strong placenta and it is the placenta which affects milk and colostrum production, lamb growth as well as the hormones which stimulate the mothering activity.

During the growing season, sheep can get all the nutrition they need from grazing as long as they are grazing well managed pastures. Remember the rule of thumb is that a ewe needs 25 pounds of lush grass per day while she is raising her lamb. Things get a little trickier once the frosts shut down grass production, but by then the lambs are weaned. It gets more difficult, but as long as the ewes are in good condition (2.5+), grazing can continue well past killing frosts into early winter.

The best gauge for a ewe's nutritional requirement is the sheep herself. And the best way to find out if the sheep needs more feed is to get your hands on her. If she's skinny, she needs more feed. If she's in good shape, you're feeding her properly.

Some shepherds with many years' experience can get a pretty close body condition scoring estimate of their own flock just by looking at the sheep. But even they don't trust their eyeball assessment. Any shepherd worth their name will always insist on getting a hands-on evaluation before deciding what shape the sheep is in and how to adjust the ration. Once you know if the ewes are fat or skinny, you'll know if they've been getting enough, too much or too little feed. Keep in mind that not all feed has the same value, and quantity does not always make up for quality.

Because of the sheep's wool cover, a hands-on body condition scoring system is the only way to find out which ewes are skinny or fat. We run the flock through a chute with a sorting gate. While they're in the chute, we get our hands on each ewe's back. That's where we find out how much or how little backbone is sticking up.

The standard body condition scoring system has a five point evaluation. If a ewe is in a #1 BCS, she's close to death from starvation. If you've got a ewe in a #5 BCS, she's so fat she has a hard time waddling to the feed trough without getting a heart attack. Most well managed commercial sheep are kept in a #2.5 to #3.5 BCS range, depending on the phase of the production cycle. Ewes that fall below #2.5 BCS are not productive. Sheep with more than #4 BCS are overfed and are generally driving up the flock's cost of production without any additional financial or management gain.

If a ewe's backbone is sticking up and feels sharp, the ewe is a #2 BCS. She's skinny and probably needs more feed, or at least a deworming. If you can still feel her backbone but it feels more like a thick finger under her hide and it isn't up very high and doesn't feel sharp or hard-edged, call her a #3 BCS. If you hit a ewe that's got a back as wide as uncle Klem's old plow horse and instead of a backbone all you feel is a dip where the backbone ought to be, call her a #4 BCS and run her with the average ewes. Keep an eye on the fat ewes to make sure they actually lamb because you can't afford too many barnyard bimbos, considering the number of politicians and senior civil servants we're already supporting.

Everyone has their own interpretation of what they feel when they press their fingers against a ewe's backbone and feel over her short ribs. The important thing is not matching what other people score your sheep, but understanding when your sheep are too skinny or too fat for the job they're supposed to be doing. Keep in mind that sheep will drop a full BCS point in two weeks of being underfed. It takes them six weeks of top notch rations to rebuild that single BCS point they lost in 14 days.

In our climate with its 200 day winter feed period, a well managed rotational pasture system can provide enough feed for every phase of the production cycle except breeding and gestation, both of which take place in mid-winter months. The only exception is when we get deep snow early in winter. This prevents most of the early winter grazing, and we begin topping off the flock with hay as soon as the snow gets too deep. Once the snow gets more than eight inches deep or forms a crust, we top off the feed with hay.

Extended season grazing takes a lot of planning and strong sheep who know how to look after themselves away from the barnyard. The most important point to remember when considering an extended winter grazing project is to ensure you have lots of quality grass under the snow. Fields for winter grazing should be allowed to grow at least an eight inch stand of grass before freeze up. The grass under the snow should be feed tested, and supplements supplied to the grazing flock as required.

Brooke Rodgerson, an experienced winter grazing manager from Minnesota, uses a quarter acre per hundred head per day ratio to estimate how much winter grazing potential a given field has. She bases her estimate on an eight inch stand of grass under the snow. To establish the feed value, she does feed tests on pasture clippings just before the flock is put in to graze.

On our operation we are not as scientific. We move the flock into a pasture which was allowed to regrow before freeze up. The sheep are turned loose and allowed to graze, but as insurance we place a few medium quality bales in the pasture. If the ewes start feeding on the bales, we either begin feeding hay or move on to another pasture. We also body condition score the ewes every two or three weeks. For added security, we track a few of our older sheep on a daily basis to see how they are doing. I also take note of how long the flock spends grazing. If they never settle down, I know it's time to feed or move on to new pastures.

Grazing in general, and winter grazing in particular, is as much instinct as it is hard and fast science. Before getting involved in a winter grazing situation, you should be very confident that you do a good job managing the summer grazing. Then just before you launch into your winter grazing project, make sure you've got enough feed on hand to take care of the sheep just in case the whole thing goes bust because of a bad storm or bad judgment on your part.

One of the best investments you can make if you're serious about understanding your flock's nutritional requirement is to buy the "Nutrition Guide for B.C. Sheep Producers". I believe it's still available from the B.C. Ministry of Agriculture and Food. It's got a lot of what at first seems to be high tech mumbo jumbo but when you read it with a grass farmer's perspective, there is a lot you'll be able to use. The only problem for me is that the whole damn thing is in metric while our farm measurements are still in imperial measurements. Make sure you've got fresh batteries in your calculator.

11

THE GRAZING FLOCK AND GUARD DOGS

*B*efore you can safely graze sheep anywhere in this country, you have to have effective predator control. In most areas, the main predator is the coyote, a skilled and persistent lamb connoisseur. There isn't an electric fence or artificial deterrent that will stop coyotes for long. This freeloading lamb thief can put you out of business quick if you don't take care of the problem before it starts. The only long term solution is to send a reformed thief to catch an active thief. The reformed thief you send has to be a predator control dog who is attentive to the flock and completely trustworthy. These dogs exist and are as essential to a sheep grazing operation as the grass.

We were losing up to 30 per cent of our lambs to predators and ready to quit when we got our first guard dog. The move was the last gasp from a dying sheep ranch in the heart of coyote country. It paid off, and keeps on paying off. But every rose has its thorns and so do predator control dogs.

Before we deal with the thorns, let's look at the benefits. Putting it all in a nutshell, the main benefit is that predator control dogs make it possible to run a grass based sheep operation. Without them or some other equally effective predator control animal constantly living with the flock, the entire sheep grazing concept is a non-starter. Even flocks under the constant supervision of an experienced rifle-toting shepherd are not as well protected as flocks under the eye of a single guard dog. And nothing, but nothing, can protect a flock better than an established pair of experienced guard dogs.

Our flock has grazed through some of the toughest brush country in the province without significant predator losses. We've had them grazing rolling prairie and parkland with the same success. We grazed our ewes, with lambs at foot, on pastures where neighbors lost 30 or more lambs a summer. Our flock didn't take any losses. After a few years, the neighbors sold their unprotected sheep. The only difference between the two flocks was that our sheep were being protected by the guard dogs. Even with the added pressure of newborn lambs and afterbirth spread over a number of pastures, the dogs still manage to keep the coyotes and bears away. They won't even allow crows and other scavenger birds to feed on the afterbirth.

Our first flock guard dog was a Great Pyrenees called Joshua. He was a bit like that Old English sheep dog you used to see on the Bugs Bunny show before they banned the cartoon violence from the tube. When we first got him, he damn near ate us out of house and home but I was too scared to cut back his feed in case he got started eating lamb. He never did, but I watched him and watched him. All he ever did was sit around all day and doze, but our predator losses dropped dramatically.

After a few years, I was beginning to wonder if we needed a dog at all because we rarely saw coyotes anymore and had hardly any losses. By this time, we had two dogs and I was seriously wondering if we'd been taken in by another fad that sweeps the sheep business every year or two. I figured that the coyote population had just died off or something.

Just to see if the dogs were doing anything at all, I decided to test them. I got all dressed up in hunting camo and waited until dusk. The idea was to see if I could sneak up to where the flock was bedded down without the dogs spotting me. The flock was about a mile from home and I walked out. I had lots of cover and made sure I kept the breeze in my face. When I got closer, I was down on my hands and knees at first and dropped to a belly crawl 200 yards from the flock. I still had plenty of cover and was confident I could make it up to the flock without getting caught.

I wanted to see what they would do if I surprised them.

Just before I dropped to a belly crawl, I made sure both dogs were still with the flock. When I checked again after crawling 15 yards, all I could see was the male and he was up and walking around with his tail up. I did not see the female. I kept crawling and took another look at about 150 yards from the flock. As soon as my head came above the cover, I heard something on my left running very hard toward me. In a flash I knew it was the bitch racing in to tackle me, because the male was now running at me full tilt barking. I jumped up a split second before the bitch got to me. The pair had set me up, not knowing what I was. They calmed down once they realized it was me, the guy who feeds and looks after them. They scared me so much that I just about had a very embarrassing accident. After that, I never question the dog food bill again.

Dogs have some very strong advantages over other guard animals such as donkeys or llamas. Dogs understand coyotes because they both operate by the same set of rules. A coyote doesn't have to see a dog to know that he's in the area. The dog's scent markings are often enough to keep the coyote away from the sheep, because the coyote will know from the scent marking that the dog is larger and aggressive about the territory. All dogs are territorial, and they will work hard to keep their territory secure. Guard dogs are more territorial than most, and they will claim and defend any territory the sheep choose to graze. That means that as long as the coyotes can avoid the sheep and the dog, it can overlap its territory with the sheep. We've found this works quite well and avoids the constant battle trying to kill every coyote in the area.

The whole thing is ecologically sound in terms of balancing the natural system with sheep ranching. Occasionally, once every five years or so, you will run into a coyote that insists on killing lambs in spite of the dogs. When this happens we move the sheep to new pastures and pull out all the stops until we kill the coyote doing the damage.

Good dogs are worth every penny you spend on them.

Now that we've discussed the beauty of the rose, it's time to deal with the thorns, and this rose has some very sharp thorns.

For every guard dog that worked out, we had one that didn't. The ones that don't give the rest a very bad reputation because they kill and maim the sheep they're supposed to be protecting. Sometimes young dogs go bad because we didn't condition them properly while they were pups. Some dogs are just not meant to guard sheep. Most of the research on the subject indicates that 50 to 60 per cent of the guard dog pups started develop into attentive trustworthy guardians. The rest just don't make the grade.

You have to have a tolerance for a certain amount of trouble when you're breaking in a young dog. It takes about 18 months to two years before the dogs settle down. In those 18 months, some dogs will show you every side of bad you can imagine. We've had dogs chew up ears, tails and entire lambs just for sport. As they got older, they began to bother ewes. We've even had one renegade who would cut a ewe out of the flock, run it into the bush, kill it and take a meal. He'd killed a couple before I got suspicious, and one more before we put him down. Most of the time, they just maul the sheep or lamb they've picked out for attention.

It's not pretty, and it definitely makes you wonder about the whole concept, especially if it's your first try at conditioning a guard dog. If I were starting out again, I would not fool with a pup or juvenile dog. I would pay the going rate and buy a mature experienced dog that has proven to be trustworthy and attentive with sheep.

Think of it as an insurance policy. You pay a fee to protect a $50,000 or $100,000 investment for five years. The mature dog will cost some serious cash, currently in the $1,000 range, but if you're paying $150 per ewe lamb replacement and lambs are worth $95 a head as feeders, you don't have to save a lot of animals before the dog has earned his purchase price. On the other hand, a $250 juvenile in training can easily kill or maim five or ten head before they settle down or get put down.

Over the years we've had 10 dogs and six turned out just fine. One of our early bitches was out of an Hungarian breed. She was a bit like Zsa Zsa Gabor in Green Acres, a Hungarian princess with a lot of show and flash but not a clue about work. She went on to become someone's pet and I think she eventually bit a police officer.

The mature pair we have now are the best so far. They remind me of the old Miami Vice show. These two are fast, flashy and fatal. We call them Sophia and Salvador and they're Maremmas. I think of them as our coyote SWAT team and they're doing far more than just earning their keep. Last summer we sent over a thousand ewes and lambs into some pretty rough and remote pastures. When we counted the lambs that fall, it was only four short of what we sent out. We lambed on pasture and we only lost one lamb to coyotes. Even then the coyote that killed the lamb never got to enjoy his meal because Salvador was sitting beside the dead lamb next morning.

I can already hear the skeptics chuckling, "You fool, it was your dog that killed the lamb." I don't think so, because it was a classic coyote lamb kill: a cracked skull and crushed larynx.

When it comes to talking about what breed is best, the best thing I've heard comes from a fellow in the States who's been doing research on flock guard dogs for more than five years. He's been looking at hundreds of dogs of all breeds and descriptions being used under working farm and ranch conditions. His conclusion is that no one breed is better than any other. The biggest factor between success and failure is the genetic background and the way the pups are conditioned.

We've been lucky. Most of our dogs have done us some good but the best dogs we've ever had are the ones we're running right now. Our neighbors on the section north of us also run sheep. They keep them near the barnyard and run goats with the sheep to keep the coyotes away. Last summer they lost over 30 lambs. I'm not saying they wouldn't have lost any lambs if they were running a dog or two to protect their sheep, but I'm sure it would have made a difference. The thing with these guard dogs is that if they don't do the job, get rid of them and get another one or two.

We run a pair partly because of the size of the flock and partly because of the country we graze. In open country one good dog could look after 1,000 or more ewes, but in bush and hill country he could use a little help. The other thing is that a male/(spayed) female pair seem to keep each other company which keeps them with the flock in the early adult stages.

Flock guard dogs are guard dogs. They're not pets or companions and they're not herding dogs. A guard dog can become an excellent pet, but a pet can never become a guard dog. Would you really expect a dog that's been pampered, petted and allowed to watch TV to move out to a barnyard with a flock of sheep. But if they've been bred properly and brought up right, they'll work out most of the time. It has to be stuck into their heads right from the start that their only function in life is to protect the sheep.

To make sure they've got a half decent chance to do their job, they've got to be conditioned and bonded to the flock when they are very young, as in just weaned. It's best to buy pups from a working sheep farm where the breeding pair has a proven record. Make sure the young dogs are not family pets when you do buy.

Our most recent pair came from a sheep farm in Minnesota. They were four months old and almost wild. The fella who was raising them told us that their mother whelped out in the sheep pasture and they didn't get to see the pups until they were out on patrol with their mother. He coaxed the bitch and her pups into the barn when he rounded up the sheep. Once he had the pups in the barn, he was able to grab them and put them into transport kennels. They got their shots and my good looking partner went to pick them up.

When she got them home, I put them into a small sheep pen beefed up with snow fence. First I turned loose Salvador. He made one loop around the pen, bit through two snow fence pickets and ran into the flock. We fixed the hole and turned loose Sophia. She went straight to the fence, snapped one picket and joined her partner among the sheep.

We thought that would probably be the last we saw of either dog. But they stayed with the flock and we knew they were eating because the dog food we set out for them was usually gone in a day or two. They've more than held up their end of the deal and under some pretty tough conditions.

The whole concept of dogs guarding sheep is a bit strange when you think about it. Dogs usually kill sheep and to have one or two ready to fight to protect the flock is a strange and somewhat twisted reality. To make it work, the shepherd has to understand that he is asking the lion to lie with the lamb and not eat it. It is being done every day on thousands of sheep

farms and ranches, but it does take a certain amount of tolerance for the dog's bad habits during the early stages. It requires patience and a firm hand, and most of all it calls for an
overwhelming desire for the concept to work. If the shepherd
has doubts about the concept or throws in the towel before
there is success, the sheep guardian dog concept will not
work. You have to be ready to accept the loss of a few lambs
and a ewe or two to make this work.

If it makes you feel better, just remember that you'd be
giving them up to the coyotes anyway. At least when you're
breaking in a dog, you've got a chance for some long term pay
back.

12

THE TRUTH ABOUT SHEEP FENCES

Fences, well planned, well built and affordable, are as important as the sheep, the dogs and the grass itself. If you can't control where your flock grazes, you can't manage the grass and if you can't manage the grass, you can't run a sheep grazing operation unless you plan to herd your flock all year. Most successful grazing outfits use some form of rotational grazing. The most successful of these usually have the best rotational grazing system which brings us back to fencing.

Sheep have a bad reputation when it comes to respecting fences. Cowboy legend has it that if you can spit over it or blow smoke through it, it'll never hold sheep. As with all legends there is some small grain of truth to it. But then cowboys never did like building fences. The first thing a good sheep pasture fence needs is lots of grass inside the fence. If the sheep still insist on busting out, it's time to do some culling. Persistent fence crawlers can cost you a lot of money and time. Identify them and cull them immediately because you don't want them leading your flock into a lush alfalfa field and bloating 50 or 60 ewes the way they did on our place. We managed to save all but ten, but it taught us a lesson. A few days later I shot and butchered the three ewes that were causing all the problems.

But even if you have grass inside the fence and a decent fence-respecting flock, there are still basically two types of sheep fences, those that hold sheep and those that don't. There is no shortage of designs that don't hold sheep. Some of the most interesting look like a barricade thrown up by a desperate soul preparing for a shoot out. The building material list can include anything movable; a kitchen sink, a bath tub or two, an old car, some old wooden freight pallets and maybe even some wire and scrap lumber. Another system, more popular for longer stretches, comes right out of a WW I manual. This fencing method involves sticking posts into the ground and then hanging as much barbed and page wire on the posts as you can find.

The old traditional page wire sheep fence will do the job. The problem is that it is very expensive and takes a lot of labor, posts and page wire to build. The only operations that can afford a page wire sheep fence today are government funded sheep research farms. Which leaves us with the multi strand, high tensile steel wire electric fence as the only viable option.

At the P&L we've been messing around with electric fencing for years and until recently we've had as many failures as successes. We recently added a half section of pasture land to our operation and I did not want a problem with the new neighbors, so I began looking around for an electric fencer (energizer) that I could count on to keep us and our sheep out of trouble. We don't have hydro at the new pasture so that added another problem. I had about a half dozen fencers of varying descriptions lying around the place but all of them have failed me at one time or another. Not one of them was reliable enough to take on seven or more miles of fence I was planning to build on this new pasture.

I got busy and built the fence using high tensile steel wire in a four wire pattern with two wires insulated to carry the power. We spaced the wire at six, eight, 10 and 12 inch spacings. I leave the bottom wire neutral and charge the next two wires. The top wire is also neutral. In high pressure areas or with more aggressive flocks, a five wire fence with slightly narrower spacings and a bit more height may be necessary. I used end springs and made sure we didn't overtighten the wire. We used two railway ties with a six to eight inch post to build "H" type strainers, corners and gate posts. I also used quality insulators and fastened the neutral wire to the posts with extra long staples.

After finishing the fence, I started talking to manufacturers' reps from the electric fencing business to find out more about electric fencers. I learned some interesting facts about electric fencers and fences.

I bought a digital electric fence tester because I could see that if I didn't know what my fencers were putting out, I really didn't know what I had at home and I really didn't want to buy another fencer. I tested all of my old fencers and found out that they didn't have the power to hold sheep in the fence.

The longer I own this digital fence tester, the more I see how important it is in maintaining and operating an electric fence system. Things can get pretty confusing when you ask fencing pros about their products. They talk about the various types and power ratings. Some fencers are rated on the miles of fence they can charge, others are rated on the voltage output and still others have a joule rating. According to the pros, the best fencer description should give you all three.

I got one of the experts to explain what each of these ratings mean. He explained that each rating is valid and accurately describes what the fencer can do. The most critical rating, the one that gives the fence its sheep control potential, is the joule rating. A joule is a unit of power, the same as horsepower only much smaller. One joule is equal to one watt for one second. The more joules, the more zap and more zap equals more stopping power. After one or two eyeball arcing encounters with the fence, even the peanut-sized brain of a sheep will understand that a fence is not a good thing to touch.

Cows and horses, being the wimps they are, will stand in total terror of a one or two joule fence. Sheep, on the other hand, should have a six or seven joule lesson anytime they come into contact with the fence. The trick is to deliver the zap to every part of the fence even when it's overgrown with brush and weeds, and for that you need a powerful energizer.

I was worried about the weeds and brush growing into our new fence line and had planned to use chemical sprays to control it. The pros advised me that it wouldn't be necessary, provided I purchase a fencer with enough power. I thought they were just trying to pry more money out of my pocket so I didn't take them seriously and continued to make plans for a fence line sprayer. Then I realized both pros representing different companies had made the same claim and I decided to call them on it.

I asked them if they were willing to let me test one of their units on my fence for a week or ten days to see how well it would perform. They both agreed. The problem was that I had to get a bigger solar panel because the units they were sending were going to take a fair bit of battery power to operate. By this time I had my best old fencer hooked to the new fence. It was getting its juice from a new ten watt solar panel which was hooked to a new battery. The system was beginning to lose quite a bit of power. When I hooked up the new high powered unit, it didn't get any better and I thought these electric fencing pros were selling me a bunch of electric bull. So I called to complain and the first thing the guy wanted to know is what type of ground rod I was using. I told him it was a three foot long chunk of re-bar pounded into the ground almost three feet.

He suggested I try a new ground rod or two set into moist ground at least six feet. I figured he was nuts, but by this time I was committed to making the fence work. Besides, I was getting sick of my dogs scratching themselves on this high tech solar powered electric fence and not getting any more than a flea bite. I pounded the ground rods into a slough along the fence and ran the top fence wire back to the fencer as my ground lead. I used the same bolt-on wire clamps as I did on the hot wires to ensure I had good connections.

Once the work was done, I hooked up the fencer and tested the line. The new readings were up where they should have been all along on every part of the fence. And, in less than an hour, each one of the dogs learned to stay away from the fence. No more haphazard re-bar ground rods for this sheep farmer. I am now a firm believer in six or seven foot galvanized ground rods as part of an electric fence system.

Once the ground rods were in place, the high power fencer did just what the rep said it would do. Over a couple of days, it cleared itself a path along the wire through the weeds. Each morning when I tested the fence, the power kept increasing until it was the same at the end of the fence as at the energizer which was at the midway point of the fence. Today when a electric fence pro tells me, "More power will never hurt your fence," I know what they're talking about.

Buying the type of fencer that can control weed growth and sheep is going to cost serious money, but so does buying five or six cheap fencers that don't get the job done. For people who think this is all too expensive, try pricing out a mile of sheep wire and four inch posts at 12 to 16 foot spacings. Then compare that to the price of a five wire barbed wire fence with posts at 16 feet. When you got all that done, price out a four wire high tensile steel wire fence with posts at 30 to 40 feet, include insulators and tension springs and you'll see why you can still afford a $1,000 energizer on a seven or eight mile rotational fencing project.

When you design the fence layout for a rotational pasture, keep in mind that sheep need lots of clean fresh water through the summer months. We've found that running an alleyway along one end of the pasture connecting all the pastures to a single water point is a real benefit. It allows you to move sheep from field to field easily and ensures that each field has a water point.

To get a better understanding of how to design and manage a rotational grazing system, take a look at books written by Allen Savory and Allen Nation on the subject. Their books should give you some ideas on how to set up your own pasture system, as well as provide a good understanding of the working principals of rotational grazing.

We also use a lot of portable electric fencing to further break down our pasture size and control the flock's grazing pattern. This portable fencing helps break down the fields even further and with them we can force the sheep to clean up grass they would normally leave behind. The portable fence or "electric netting" is also very handy in our drift lambing program. It allows us to again break up pastures and control the flock's movement at a time when we want to keep the new pairs separate from the drop band. There are two types: netting and mesh. The netting, 100 yards for $160, is a three or four wire set up complete with steel tipped plastic posts. You can carry 100 yards easily under your arm and set it up in less than 10 minutes. We currently have about a 1,000 yards of this portable fencing.

For sheep that aren't trained yet or a bit harder to control, you might have to use electric mesh. This is, as the name implies, a netting similar to page wire, but with smaller spacings. It is completely electrified and comes complete with its own posts. It is much more expensive, costing about $150 per 50 yards. It is also lightweight and fairly long lasting. We've used our hot mesh for five years and made only minor repairs. We use the portable fencing to subdivide existing pastures and to hold them overnight when we're stubble grazing or on short term lease land.

At first blush all this high tech fencing sounds pretty costly but this is one place where technology can actually make you money in a sheep operation. It's all worth it because once the perimeter and cross fencing is in place you can get even more control with portable fencing which you can move around all over the place. Once you're set up, all you have to do is go out, test the line with your handy dandy digital fence tester and watch the lambs learn to respect the fence. Around here we like checking fences so much my partner and I occasionally drive out to the sheep pasture just to watch the sun set over the flock safely inside the electric fence. It may not be romantic from an urban point of view but it works for us.

13

SHEEP DOGS AND WORKING CORRALS

*S*heep dogs and working corrals are integral parts of any sheep operation. Trying to manage a grazing flock without a good dog or two is a hopeless cause. Trying to sort, vaccinate, deworm or body condition score a commercial flock without a good working corral simply can't be done.

Trying to move sheep and control the flock's movements without the help of a good dog is hopeless. Even if you can run like the wind it's still a frustrating experience. Most people give up and resort to the "grain bucket herding" technique. Even with the flock following you and your grain bucket, you still don't have control and sooner or later some sheep will get tired of following you and you have to start all over again. After a while most people simply give up and declare in a loud voice to anyone who'll listen that sheep are too dumb to handle.

If you're going to run sheep on pasture, you have to be able to control the flock whenever and wherever the need comes up. The only way to do that is with a good dog or two or three. If you aren't familiar with sheep dogs or haven't been able to train one yourself, buy a trained dog. You'll need it if you're going to run sheep. Trying to run a commercial sheep farm without a competent dog is like trying to run a grain farm without a seeder.

I'm not going to try to explain how to train a dog; there are lots of good books and videos on the subject. My suggestion is that if you don't know anything about dogs, buy your first one fully trained. That way the only one in the team who'll have to learn what to do when is the shepherd and if they can't read they sure can watch a video. Make sure you know how to control the dog and if you're not sure, get the trainer to give you lessons as part of the dog's purchase price.

If you buy a dog and train it yourself and it ends up a complete wreck, the whole idea of a herding dog as an essential tool begins to get smelly. But, if your first experience with a herding dog is positively wonderful and the mutt does everything but shear the flock, you'll understand why so many sheep people would sooner lose body parts than their dogs.

Once you and the dog have figured out who does what, you'll be able to bring the sheep into the working corral without working up a sweat. If you don't have good working corrals, you'll never manage the workload no matter how good the dog. You can't manage a commercial flock unless you can handle 600 or 700 head in an afternoon, and you can't do that by dragging each sheep out of the corral to vaccinate and deworm it. You can't manage a commercial flock if every time you need to sort out a few fats or skinny sheep, you have to round up a dozen neighbors just to get the job done. The key to good flock management is to get the job that needs doing done on time with the least amount of effort.

A lot of sheep operations hit a wall because they simply cannot cope with the amount of work it takes to process more than 200 sheep. It is possible for two people and their dogs to vaccinate and deworm up to 1,000 sheep in eight hours. It's also possible to do this without working yourself to death. On our place three of us and our three dogs have completed a three step processing operation on 500 ewes in less than three hours. We can sort a 1,500 head flock into three groups in under two hours. The key to handling this many sheep is corral design supported by good stockmanship and decent dogs.

Corral design and stockmanship both require a good understanding of sheep psychology. The first thing a person has to understand to work sheep using a dog is that the sheep are afraid of the dog but they are not afraid of people. So let the dog gather the sheep and herd them to you. Once the dog has gathered the sheep, it will drive the flock to where you are. Stay ahead of the flock and lead them into the yards and the dog should keep the flock following behind you. Remember if you try to drive sheep the way you chase cattle, you're only making work for yourself and your dog.

You can move cows quite easily by getting somewhere behind the herd and walking towards them. If you try that with sheep, they may or may not bunch up but it's unlikely that they'll begin to move in a predictable direction. Most of the time they'll either mill around or race off somewhere. If you let the dog do the gathering and have it herd the sheep toward you, the operation will proceed smoothly.

Be patient, give the dog time to gather the flock. Don't over command the dog, let it work. It probably knows more about moving sheep than you do anyway. Sometimes it takes two or three attempts before the dog gets enough control over the sheep to move them where they have to go. Encourage the dog to try again if it fails and be careful not to discourage it from trying again. Lots of dogs have simply quit working because they got sick of being yelled at every time they started out to gather the flock.

I know of what I speak, I've screwed up more times than my dog before he finally taught me to be patient. It got to the point between us that if I raised my voice, he'd take off into the bush and hide. Eventually I learned to give him time to do the job without screaming my lungs out at him.

Once you get the sheep to the working corral, make sure you've got plenty of swinging gates dividing up the long narrow holding pens. Trying to manage a large flock of sheep without breaking them up into small manageable groups is impossible.

We use what the New Zealanders and Australians call a "bugle race". It's a corral that takes advantage of the flock's milling tendency. Sheep instinctively turn back into the flock as soon as they get confused or pressured, so any corral system that allows them to do this works much better. In our corral the flock comes into a long pen, about twenty feet wide, 100 feet long. This pen flows into the bugle which is divided in two, splitting the flock. The bugle narrows down to a chute. At every stage there are swinging gates to divide the flock into smaller groups. This controls the amount of movement, limits the crushing effect and makes moving groups much simpler. The sheep flow into this system easily because they think they are going back into the flock as they come around the turn in the bugle. We can easily control the smaller groups once the gates divide the flock because they too think they're escaping back into the flock.

Once the sheep are all inside the corral and the gates are closed, the best way to work the sheep forward is to walk into the bunch from the front. As you walk toward the group, the sheep will rush past you to escape. If you try to drive them forward from behind, you'll scare a few of the sheep immediately in front of you and they'll try to get behind you but you won't make an impression on the sheep at the front and they're the ones who have to go through the gate. So go to the gate in front, open it and walk towards the sheep. They will run past you thinking they're escaping and end up in the next pen which is where they were supposed to go.

We use five to six inch pressure treated posts and one inch lumber for our corrals. The posts are set at four foot spacings and the fence is at least 40 inches high. All the gates are hinged and made of one inch square tubing frames with weld mesh fill. This makes for a strong gate and allows the sheep to see through the gate. Sheep will not move easily towards a solid wall even if it is a gate. It helps to build the corral so the sheep can see the rest of the flock as they make the turn in the bugle part of the system. It also helps to make the outside fence of the bugle solid to prevent movement outside the corral from distracting the sheep as they move through the system.

The chute itself should have solid walls on both sides with the cut off and end gates made of see-through material. We like to have our working chute long enough to hold 35 or 40 ewes. To make sure we don't end up with ewes injured in the chute, it is divided into two or three sections using cut off gates. The gates again break up the sheep making them easier to manage.

The location of sheep yards is almost as important as their design. If you can't use the yards because it's too muddy or windy or because it's drifted with snow, it's no good to you. Take your time and plan your working corral properly. Build it well and it'll serve you for many years. Once you've got the corral built and the sheep are familiar with it, they'll move through it much faster. We often put the flock through the system without doing anything to them just so they'll know how to get out of it. The best way is to pen the whole flock and then leave the gates open so they can walk themselves out through the chute. If you walk away, they'll all file out as nice as can be and the next time they go through the system things will go a lot easier.

14

SHARP PENCIL SHEEP FARMING

The key to long term survival in any business is profit. It's the same in the sheep business. The problem with the sheep business is that not enough people see record keeping and cost control as part of the farm workload. It's as important as any other farm work. If you don't know what things are costing you or how much you are earning, you're just fumbling in the dark. Fumble in the dark long enough and you're going to run into problems.

You can't hold a flock responsible for poor management decisions which created a debt the flock can't support. Each operation will through its own strengths and weaknesses pay less or more in production costs. The point to remember when you are working out your cost projections and cash flow sheets is that lamb prices are at the low part of the market cycle far longer than they are at the high part. That means you have to keep your production costs at a level where you are still making a profit when lamb prices dip to the bottom of the price cycle. If you can keep your cash production costs in the $35 to $40 per ewe per year range through the late 1990s and market a 140 to 150 per cent lamb crop you should be alright. You'll be all right as long as you don't saddle the flock with huge debt repayments or expect a couple hundred sheep to give you $30,000 a year spending money. If you keep things sensible, you'll prosper when prices are strong and easily survive market downturns.

If all this talk about bookkeeping work is too much for you and you figure you'll be alright without it, you're wrong. If you can't do it yourself, hire someone to do it, but get it done. Once you know your production costs, keep a tight grip on your check book because I've let my grip slip from time to time and our production costs shot through the roof.

If you keep your costs in line and adapt the fundamentals of grass farming to your sheep enterprise you'll be amazed how profitable these wooly mortgage lifters can be.

The best advice anyone ever gave me on how to make a go of the sheep business was, "Look after your sheep and they'll look after you." It took a while for me to understand what that fine old gentleman was trying to tell me but I think I'm beginning to work it out.